Empowered by Choice

Women of Confidence

SERIES

Empowered *by* Choice

Positive Decisions Every Woman Can Make

KENDRA SMILEY

SERVANT PUBLICATIONS
ANN ARBOR, MICHIGAN

Vine Books is an imprint of Servant Publications especially designed to serve evangelical Christians.

Published by Servant Publications
P.O. Box 8617
Ann Arbor, Michigan 48107

99 00 01 02 03 5 4 3 2 1

Printed in the United States of America
ISBN 1-56955-070-0

LIBRARY OF CONGRESS CATALOGING-IN-PUBLICATION DATA

Smiley, Kendra, 1952-
Empowered by choice : positive decisions every woman can make / Kendra Smiley.
p. cm. — (Women of confidence series)
Includes bibliographical references.
ISBN 1-56955-070-0 (alk. paper)
1. Christian women—Religious life. 2. Attitude (Psychology)—Religious aspects—Christianity. I. Title. II. Series.
BV4527.S6 1998
248.8'43—dc21 98-19600
CIP

DEDICATION

To my husband, John,
an encourager who has modeled Christ to me
for more than thirty years.

Contents

Foreword

Have you ever had to deal with depressing situations or dilemmas that would not disappear? Have you often felt dejected, deflated, and demoralized? Of course you have! Not a day goes by that we all don't have to face some of life's difficulties.

In her book, Kendra introduces us to women who share their real-life experiences, women with whom we can relate. She presents us with their stories, which like beautifully wrapped gifts, each bring a ray of personal hope and encouragement. You'll laugh and cry when you read about these women who refused to let life's circumstances destroy their positive attitudes.

Kendra is an exciting new talent with a delightful writing and speaking style. I know you will enjoy reading and being motivated as I was by Kendra's message of choosing a positive attitude for life.

Florence Littauer
Author of over twenty books including
Personality Plus, Silver Boxes, and
It Takes So Little to Be Above Average

Acknowledgements

This is the spot where I have the opportunity to recall and recognize all of the people who have helped with this adventure. Family first—my husband, John, and our three sons, Matthew, Aaron, and Jonathan, were and are a great source of encouragement to me. They are all overflowing with life and love. They make me laugh and they keep me accountable (two very important things). Thanks to all four of them for providing me with ample material and for permitting me to use it.

Pam, my right- and left-hand woman, has far exceeded any possible expectations for helpfulness and patience. She is more than an office assistant, she is a dear friend and counselor. Thank you to Pam.

Thanks to all the women who allowed me to tell their stories. It was not an easy task to reduce their experiences, courage, and good choices into one chapter each. I am grateful that these women are in my life.

I am also grateful for my girlfriends at church. They have cheered me on for many years, letting me practice my delivery on them, being patient with my "creative" (that means disorganized) side, and actually convincing me that they *want* to hear me give a message or to read what I have written.

Thanks to the teenagers in our Bible studies who have checked on my progress periodically and prayed with and for me. They were the ones who reminded me not to put off my writing and end up having to "pull an all-nighter."

Thank you to my husband's brother, Wynn. He is an amazingly creative gentleman who is always willing to listen to a new idea and to help me refine and develop it.

And finally—thanks to Gwen Ellis, my editor at Servant Publications. I think her most frequent statement was, "You can do it!" (And when you are writing a book for the Women of Confidence series, that is very important!) I *did* do it, but largely because of her mentoring and her belief that I could.

And of course, thank you, Jesus, for saving my soul. Thank you, Jesus, for making me whole.

1

If Only

Don't be discouraged;
everyone who got where he is,
started where he was.
Author unknown

Watch for big problems;
they disguise big opportunities.
Author unknown

It was 7:15 on a beautiful Sunday morning. I was sitting at the island in our kitchen having a cup of tea when the phone rang.

"Good morning," I said cheerfully.

The caller was hesitant. Finally a muffled voice sobbed into the receiver.

"Kendra," the man said emotionally, "this is Steve. Pam asked me to call you."

Pam is a dear friend and sister in Christ. Our distant locations and busy lives prohibit frequent visits, but we stay in touch by phone calls and letters.

My mind raced as I tried to determine what had prompted this tearful call. Something was wrong and I literally held my breath as he continued.

"It's about Emily," Steve continued.

Emily was their new baby, their third daughter, and she was just four months old. She obviously was in trouble, but what was wrong? My mind began to race again, now picturing Emily in each of the possible events that might have triggered the call.

"We need you to pray," Steve sobbed. "She was just diagnosed with an inoperable brain tumor."

For a moment I was too shocked to respond. In all my imagining, I had not thought of this happening. How was this possible? How could someone so young and so innocent have a condition considered by medical experts to be so impossible?

"What? Tell me more," I replied. Secretly I hoped that I had not heard him correctly ... that I had misunderstood his words and his tone.

"Emily has been having problems for about three weeks. We have had her examined by several physicians and up until this point they had no clue as to the problem. Just this morning it was determined that her illness is the result of a brain tumor," Steve explained with patience and with pain.

"Why can't they take it out? Why did you say it was inoperable?" I asked, still unable to grasp what I was hearing.

"It is a vascular tumor, one surrounded with blood vessels. If they remove it, they are sure that Emily will bleed to death," he said, and then began to sob once again.

Steve, the father of this critically ill baby, had been sent to the phone to call a list of prayer warriors. My name was just one on the list.

> When one door of happiness closes, another opens; but often we look so long at the closed door that we do not see the one that has been opened for us.
>
> *Helen Keller*

> There is little difference in people, but that little difference makes a big difference. The little difference is attitude. The big difference is whether it is positive or negative.
>
> *W. Clement Stone*

It was February and time once again for the Sunday school convention. Each year for several years, Shirley and I had helped at the convention and had shared a hotel room.

It was always a treat to be with Shirley. Her wit and

enthusiasm made our job at the booth fun and our time off even more enjoyable. She was a good friend and a mentor to me in my faith.

During a particularly long break, Shirley and I went to our hotel room to rest and talk. The convention was going well. Book sales were ringing in, and we had been having fun.

We took off our shoes, got as comfortable as we could on the hotel furniture, and started to visit. We talked about Shirley's two teenage kids—about their plans and their futures—and about my younger kids. We talked about how spectacular our husbands were and how fortunate we were. We laughed and we cried. There was nothing unusual in our doing these things, except that possibly we laughed a little less than usual and cried a little more.

This was, you see, a monumental day in Shirley's life. It was not monumental in the sense of accomplishment or rewards. It was monumental in another way. When we got to our room that afternoon, before we shared our thoughts and our dreams with one another, Shirley combed her hair and it began to fall out in handfuls from her recent chemotherapy.

Shirley had gone to the hospital recently to have a benign lump removed and had instead undergone a radical mastectomy. Her chemotherapy had begun, and after only one session she was losing her hair. Shirley was prepared for her hair loss in a practical way. She had a wig for public events and a turban for private moments. But she was not prepared in an emotional sense.

We cried together as we mourned the physical losses Shirley had already endured and thought of the many events yet to come that were too precious for Shirley to miss.

When written in Chinese,
the word "crisis" is composed of two characters
— one represents danger
and the other represents opportunity.
Author unknown

When you can't change
the direction of the wind,
adjust your sails.
Max DePree

"I got married with a very idealistic view of marriage," Betty reflected. "You know, the little house with the white picket fence … and everybody living happily ever after. By the time I realized that this wasn't true in my case and I admitted to myself that my husband was not only an unbeliever (contrary to what he had told me prior to the wedding) but was also physically abusive, I already had children. I wanted them to experience as much of an ideal atmosphere as possible, and making sure they did became my mission. I could not worry about the things I could not change.

"I remember lying in my bed one night and realizing Pete was not going to be the father he was supposed to be. I knew that, and I knew I had to go forward and do what I could to be a good mother to my children. I wanted them to have a Christian home and a church to belong to. I realized that in the spiritual sense, I was responsible for these young lives. I needed to teach them the ways of the Lord and bring them the gospel. That was *my* responsibility. I also had to understand that I was not responsible for my husband's salvation or his parenting. So I said to God, 'I'll be their mother, but you're going to have to be their Father. They don't have a father who will pray with them or read the Bible to them or teach them about you. You are going to have to father them. I'm not going to worry. I know you will meet their needs.'"

> Life's disappointments
> are life's hidden appointments.
> *Author unknown*

What do all of these real-life stories have in common? Steve and Pam faced a life-and-death situation with their baby daughter; Shirley was battling cancer; Betty found herself in an unhealthy, unhappy marriage. The common thread is that each situation had the potential to be a big "if only." If only our daughter was not so ill.... If only my health was restored.... If only I had a loving husband.... If only ...

"If only's" have existed since ancient times. In Old Testament days, Joseph had a lengthy list of possible "if only's." Remember his story? Joseph's father, Jacob, preferred him over his brothers. He was Dad's favorite, and to illustrate this fact, Jacob gave Joseph a stunning coat of many colors. His older brothers were jealous, and they threw him into a pit and then sold him into slavery.

Do we have enough potential "if only's" yet? There were more. Joseph was taken to a foreign land by the slave traders. There he diligently served Potiphar, the second in command of the nation. Potiphar's wife propositioned Joseph, and when he resisted, she lied and claimed he had assaulted her. Joseph was thrown into prison for an unspecified sentence, with no appeals.

If only he had been given a lighter jail sentence. If only Potiphar's wife had been truthful. If only she had been attracted to the gardener instead. If only the slave traders had taken a different route that day. If only Joseph's brothers had thrown him into a creek or a stream. If only Jacob had made several coats of many colors. Joseph's list of "if only's" was quite long.

Now let's take a look at Esther. Here is another Old Testament star who had plenty of opportunities for "if only's." A quick review reminds us that Esther was a beautiful young woman raised in Persia by her cousin Mordecai. At a young age she was chosen by the king to be his wife. This position was not all glitz and glamour, however. The king had some pretty frightening traditions. For example, if someone entered his chamber without being called, the king had the option of recognizing him with the extension of his scepter, or ignoring him, which meant "off with his (or her) head."

Haman, the king's right-hand man, had an intense dislike for the Jews. After Esther's cousin Mordecai refused to bow to Haman (or to anyone else but God), Haman's self-proclaimed mission became the annihilation of the Jews. Through trickery, he was able to convince the king to sanction his plan for Jewish destruction. Neither man knew that the queen was a Jew.

The plot thickened, until ultimately, Mordecai insisted Queen Esther enter the king's chambers with a plan to stop Haman. (Remember that if she was not officially recognized by the king, she would not have to worry about repeating the mistake.)

If only Mordecai had another plan. If only Esther could find someone else to stop Haman's evil. If only the king were a little more tolerant of unannounced visitors. If only she weren't the queen of Persia. The list goes on and on.

Do you have an "if only" in your life? If only your parents had appreciated your talent as much as they did your brother's. If only your father hadn't left your mother. If only your mother hadn't been an alcoholic. If only your income were greater. If only you didn't live in ____________ (fill in the blank). If only your husband were more affectionate. If only you were taller, or smaller, or slimmer, or trimmer, or wittier, or prettier. If only you weren't divorced or widowed. If only you weren't alone....

We could go on and on. There is an unending list of possible "if only's." Some of them we have created ourselves. (If only you hadn't married Fred.) Some are beyond our control. (If only you weren't the firstborn child.) Some are seemingly insignificant (if only your garage were bigger) and some are monumental (if only you could conceive a child).

An "if only" has the potential to assume a tremendous amount of power. If unleashed, an "if only" can overtake our attitudes and control our choices. The good news is that we can choose whether to give the "if only" control.

Joseph had a lot of "if only's" from which to choose. Any of those things could have justified Joseph's having a bad attitude, being jealous, or lacking confidence. But Joseph chose not to allow the "if only's" to dictate his attitude. He made the choice *not* to let the "if only's" control his future.

Esther requested that the Jewish community join her in prayer and fasting for three days before she approached the king. She did not dwell on her "if only's." She did not let them control her actions, attitudes, or confidence. She was not gripped by fear. Instead she chose not to worry and to believe, with her cousin, Mordecai, that perhaps she was made queen for just such a circumstance.

Do you want your circumstances, your "if only's," to control your attitude and rule your life? Or do you want to make choices that can lead to a positive attitude?

I know *my* answer to these questions. If I chose to, I could make a pretty impressive list of "if only's" of my own. Unpleasant things have happened in my life from time to time—"if only's" that could justify a bad attitude. Rather than let these things control my life and create a bad attitude, however, I prefer to make choices that will result in a positive attitude. Choices for a positive attitude are much more productive and much more pleasant than those that let the "if only's" take control.

After speaking to a group of gourmet cooks several years ago (not about cooking, but about working with people), I acquired a wonderful recipe for garlic bread sticks. I must pause at this point and tell you how I define "wonderful recipe." It must, first, taste good and, second, involve very little work but give the illusion that I am a good cook. This particular recipe met both criteria and it looked great too! It was a wonderful recipe.

We were having a potluck for our Sunday school class the very next week. Traditionally, I determine what I will bring to a potluck by frantically running to the pantry an hour before the event and trying to decide what I can make with what I have on hand. I, by the way, am unique in that way within my church. Most of my girlfriends are spectacular cooks. (My definition of spectacular cooks: The dish they bring to the potluck not only tastes good but also looks like it could be photographed for *Better Homes and Gardens.*)

I decided that this time I would actually plan ahead. I purchased the ingredients for the garlic bread sticks, followed the recipe, and prepared them (in bulk) as my offering for the evening. When we arrived at the potluck I unobtrusively placed my bread sticks in the long line of delicious food. Almost everyone sampled them.

"Ooooo! These bread sticks are delicious! Barb, did you bring these?"

"No? Loretta, did you make these great bread sticks?"

"You didn't? Sue, are these from your kitchen?"

This questioning continued until finally I couldn't stand it.

"Someone ask me if I made the bread sticks," I demanded. At first no one responded. I guess they were in shock at the thought.

Finally, in disbelief, someone asked, "Kendra, did *you* make the bread sticks?"

By then everyone had guessed the answer to the question. Yes, I had made the bread sticks. You see, I had a good recipe with quality ingredients and I chose to follow it.

Although I am no culinary wizard, I have learned through twenty-five years of marriage and raising a family that with a good recipe (which I actually follow) even *I* can be a good cook.

So read on and I will share with you several choices you can make to maintain a positive attitude. These choices are like the ingredients in a wonderful recipe, but, just like my famous bread stick recipe, you must use the specified ingredients and you must follow the recipe.

We'll see how Steve and Pam, Shirley, Betty, and many

others have made choices that have resulted in a positive attitude in spite of their circumstances, and in spite of their "if only's."

You, too, can triumph over your "if only's," and you can make choices that will lead to a positive attitude.

> Forgetting what is behind
> and straining toward
> what is ahead, I press on.
> *Philippians 3:13b,14a*

> The good news is
> that the bad news
> can be turned into good news
> when you change your attitude!
> *Robert Schuller*

2

Choose to Forgive

Forgiveness ought to be like a concealed
note—torn in two, and burned up,
so that it never can be shown against one.
Henry Ward Beecher

Be kind and compassionate to one another,
forgiving each other, just as in Christ
God forgave you.
Ephesians 4:32

Unforgiveness does a great deal more damage
to the vessel in which it is stored
than the object on which it is poured.
Author unknown

I grew up in a small town in the middle of America, the youngest of three children. We had a very upright home, and the standards for honesty, justice, morality, and language were high. It was not, however, a Christian home. Church did not play a significant part in our family life.

My father was a dentist and a pillar of the community (whatever that is). My mom was a homemaker. Like most married couples, they were as different as night and day. Mom was raised in an affluent, bilingual, German-American home. She was very regimented in her life. To this day, if she buys my sister a blouse for Christmas that costs $30 and gets me a robe for $29.95, she wants to tape the nickel difference to the tag.

Dad grew up in an impoverished situation. When he decided to go to dental school in the early 1930s, his parents sent him off to school with a handshake. That's all they could afford to give him.

In order to pay for dental school, he red-capped at Union Station, carrying bags for the passengers on the trains. Occasionally he could not afford to continue immediately into the next semester, but was forced to work for a few months instead. After he finally graduated, he helped his younger brother complete dental school.

Dad's dental office was very old-fashioned. There is a great possibility that many of you have never been inside an office like my dad's. The front door was a screen door on a spring. Attached at the top of the door was a little cowbell that clanged as the door banged shut. It was there to greet you and to let Dad and his assistant know that a patient had arrived. Down the hall was Dad's operating room. The chair was made of steel and had very little padding. No recliners for this office. (The recliners in dentists' offices today seem to tell you that you will be relaxed and will have a great time. At least Dad's chair didn't lie.) The light above the chair was big and glaring, blinding you into submission.

Dad was a left-handed dentist. He contended that they had no provision for teaching left-handed dentists at the time he was learning. This meant he maneuvered himself into a very awkward position as he stood at the right-handed chair. He reached across his patients and simulated half a bear hug. Furthermore, he was shaped a little like I have been on three occasions in my life—right before the birth of each of my three sons. This meant that as he examined your teeth, he gave you half a hug and you rested your ear on his tummy. (I found it very comforting and did not realize it was unusual in the least, until I had a skinny, right-handed dentist.)

Dad's office was old-fashioned, his technique was old-fashioned, and so was his generosity. Dad was hardworking and generous, maybe generous to a fault.

Dad practiced dentistry long before the establishment of medicare and federal assistance. The basic philosophy at his dental practice went something like this: "If you have a toothache, you need a dentist. I am a dentist. I'll do everything I can do to help you, and later we'll figure out how you can pay for it." Pretty generous, huh?

When my sister and brother were young Dad had a patient who paid for her dental work in live chickens. These were delivered to our home (in town!), where my dad swiftly chopped off their heads. Rumor has it that there was more than one nightmare resulting from that payment.

I don't remember the chickens, but I do recall the woman who paid for her dentures in raspberries. I realize that raspberries are expensive, but according to my calculations, she should still be bringing raspberries to my father's heirs each year.

It didn't matter to Dad. He didn't keep score. He was generous and fun and kind. And he was also an alcoholic. I always like to make sure that I present some of the positive things about Dad before I let people know that last piece of information.

Maybe you are the way I used to be. I had some real misconceptions about alcoholism. First of all, I thought alcoholics didn't live in small towns; they lived in metropolitan areas—big cities. Their addresses were something like 234 S. Skid Row. Alcoholics weren't professionals. Weren't they usually unemployed? Alcoholics definitely were not "pillars of the community." They didn't have nice families. Their kids didn't go to college. And they all drank some mysterious liquor from a container hidden in a paper bag. Is this what you think, too? Wrong!

Alcoholics live in small towns and in big cities—on Country Club Boulevard and on Skid Row. They are doctors and lawyers and teachers and plumbers and construction workers. They are employed, unemployed, and the employers. They are pillars of the community and drifters. Alcoholics have nice families and no families. Their kids are like any other kids. And alcoholics drink bargain basement liquor and the fancy stuff too.

Alcoholics are brothers and fathers and sons and mothers and sisters and daughters and grandfathers and grandmothers and nephews and nieces and husbands and wives. In fact, as you read this sentence today, there is a 25 percent chance that alcoholism has personally touched your life in some way.

If it has, you know exactly what I mean when I tell you my stomach would knot at the slightest whiff of alcohol. It didn't even have to be hard liquor. My husband has declared more than once that I could detect a teaspoon of "near beer" on the breath of a passerby.

Maybe I can. You get conditioned to things like that when you live with an alcoholic. You can also learn to become a master of denial. Denial is a skill that I developed to a very high level. I was so good at it, in fact, that I would not even admit the existence of the alcohol problem in our home. "Experts who treat alcoholism say that those people who are closest to an alcoholic are the least likely to acknowledge the existence of the alcoholism."[1]

I didn't acknowledge it until the day my husband brought it up. We had been married about three months and were living far from our childhood homes, thanks to the United States Air Force. One evening, we entertained another couple we had met at the Base Chapel. The couple was very nice and it was fun to get to know them a little better. During the course of the evening, the man told us his mother was coming for a visit. He went on in his story to tell us that she was an alcoholic. After they left, John and I talked.

"Isn't it sad that Brian's mom is an alcoholic?" I asked, sympathetically.

John looked at me with disbelief. "Your dad is an alcoholic," he said.

I was shocked and hurt. "He is not! And don't you ever say that again!" I replied.

That ended the conversation, but it started me thinking. For the first time in my life, I contemplated the possibility that my father was an alcoholic. Little by little I started to read articles and books about alcoholism. The more I learned, the more I realized the truth in John's statement. Dad was an alcoholic.

The reality of that statement was powerful. Simultaneous to this amazing admission of the truth of my dad's alcoholism came an awakening of faith in Jesus Christ in my life. The combination was practically volatile.

Now that I was a Christian and knew the reality of Christ's love, I was eager to share the truth with Dad. After all, I reasoned, he needed Jesus more than anyone I had ever known. (Please forgive my shaky theology. In reality, all people have a desperate need for Jesus, regardless of their drinking habits. Alcoholism is a very sad disease that negatively affects many others besides the diseased, but Dad was not going to hell any faster than the sober man who did not know Christ as his Savior.)

Before long I had the perfect opportunity to share my newfound faith. John's schedule in the military was rigorous and he was gone from home a great deal. After much prayer, he and I made the decision that I would return home for the last semester of his training and that I would enroll for another semester toward my college degree.

Mom and Dad were agreeable to having their empty nest filled once again, and so I went home. My mission was twofold: to finish one more semester at the university and to share the gospel with my father.

I was soon to learn that the first part of my mission was the easier part. I commuted to school each day and spent my free time between classes cramming in the library. Then each evening I would return to my parents' home and to the second part of my mission.

My prayer was a simple one: "Lord, change Dad." Fortunately, at some point I paused long enough in my requesting to listen to God. No, there was no audible voice, it was more like a thought—a thought that was bigger than any I could have had on my own. It was as though God's idea was different than mine.

"Lord, change Dad," I prayed.

The response seemed to be, *Let's not worry about your dad. Let me change you.*

"How ridiculous! I am not the one who is drinking. I

have asked you to be my Savior. I'm not the one with the problem, it's obviously Dad," I countered.

Let me change you. The response was always the same.

The thought was a novel one to me. I was very young in my faith, and yet I was growing. I didn't know much, but I did realize I was not as smart as God. So with a wavering confidence, I agreed to plan "B." No longer did I pray, "Lord, change Dad." Now instead I prayed for the willingness to let God change me.

It was difficult for me to break old patterns of behavior. I had chosen through the years to be a delightful daughter when my dad was sober, and to be a sarcastic smart aleck when he had been drinking. I was growing in my faith, and the more I read the Bible, the more I realized that there was no room for me to be a smart aleck. The truth was that I might be the only Bible Dad would ever read.

So, with God's help, I started to unlearn behavior I had perfected over the years. Each evening I would set aside some time to visit with Dad about my day. It was easy to do this on the days that he was sober. Remember, my dad was really a fun guy. The days when he had been drinking were a real challenge. I hated it when he repeated stories again and again. I hated it when he slurred his words. I hated it when he stumbled and tottered.

In order to help me curb my tongue, I developed a little trick. When my dad had been drinking and I had the urge to answer him with a rude retort, instead I clenched my fists and dug my fingernails into the palms of my hands. The self-inflicted pain had the desired effect. It reminded me to be kind and polite even when I didn't want to.

My plan worked well and I was able to be calm and courteous in my visits with Dad each evening. God was truly changing my responses. He was also changing my attitude. One night when I returned to my bedroom after my daily visit with my father, I noticed that the palms of my hands were not dented from my routine fingernail reminders. It was an interesting discovery, and I remember thinking how nice it was that Dad had changed. Then I glanced across the hall to his room and saw there had been very little change in his behavior. He had been drinking that evening and the evidence was obvious.

What had changed? Why didn't I have to dig my fingernails into my palms to control my tongue? The answer was as simple as the prayer I had uttered. God was changing me.

On that evening, the realization that my palms were unmarked was a rite of passage for me. My attitude had officially shifted. Instead of striving to alter Dad's behavior, I realized my job was to love him as Christ did. It wasn't always easy, but for the first time in my life I knew it was possible.

The semester passed (and so did I) and it was time to close that chapter of my life. It had been a time of tremendous healing for me. My father and I had experienced some degree of reconciliation in our relationship, and God was at work in both of our lives.

The significance of that time together increased greatly

when, less than a year and a half later, my father died of stomach cancer. God had allowed me to love my father—first as an act of my will, and then truly as a supernatural gift from him. That was the beginning of choosing to forgive.

You see, when you live with someone who is afflicted with the disease of alcoholism, you can accumulate many things that require forgiveness. It can take years of divine intervention before you even feel like forgiveness is making a difference. Do not grow weary. God is very explicit about our choice to forgive.

"Our Father, who art in heaven, hallowed be thy name. Thy kingdom come, thy will be done, on earth as it is in heaven. Give us this day our daily bread. And forgive us our trespasses as we forgive those who trespass against us."

In this prayer, we ask God to forgive us in the same manner we forgive others. We may be tempted to think, "But they don't deserve my forgiveness." Yet, I don't see a provision made for that attitude.

One of the saddest phrases I have ever heard uttered is "I can never forgive him." It would be more truthful to say, "I choose not to forgive him." It's still incredibly sad.

Jesus instructs us on the more perfect choice. "'Lord, how many times shall I forgive my brother when he sins against me? Up to seven times?' Jesus answered, 'I tell you, not seven times, but seventy-seven times'" (Matthew 18:21). Again there is no exception. God's instructions are not always easy, but they are always best. The first step in forgiveness is realizing that it is God's command and his desire for us. The next step is realizing that it is *our* choice.

My choice of forgiveness began as an act of my will, a choice. There is no doubt in my mind that God's Holy Spirit prompted that choice. I had the ability to listen to God's Spirit and to the Word of God or to reject it. I had the choice.

I chose to be kinder in word and deed to my father. At first I needed a crutch, the pain my fingernails inflicted on the palms of my hands each time I wanted to reply in a manner less than Christlike. But eventually, I was able to respond to Dad in a kindly manner without the painful reminder.

The gospel that I presented to my father was one with very few words. I looked for opportunities to share my faith, but moreover, I took the opportunities provided to share my love for Christ and for my father. When he died, my heart was at peace, knowing that God had worked change in me.

In my mind, that was the end of the story. I had no intention of sharing with others the story of my childhood or my reconciliation with my dad. Then about four years after my father died, I enrolled in a class for speakers—a class structured to help laypeople articulate their faith, from the pulpit and in their daily lives. I felt a prompting to write a message sharing the story of the intervention of my heavenly Father in my relationship with my earthly father. The most amazing thing occurred as I prepared that message.

As I prayed and searched the Scriptures in preparation for

my assignment, the Word of God leapt off the page.

> If anyone has caused grief [Dad], he has not so much grieved me as he has grieved all of you, to some extent—not to put it too severely. The punishment inflicted on him by the majority is sufficient for him. Now instead, you ought to forgive and comfort him, so that he will not be overwhelmed by excessive sorrow. I urge you, therefore, to reaffirm your love for him. The reason I wrote you was to see if you would stand the test and be obedient in everything. If you forgive anyone, I also forgive him. And what I have forgiven—if there was anything to forgive—I have forgiven in the sight of Christ for your sake, in order that Satan might not outwit us. For we are not unaware of his schemes.
>
> 2 Corinthians 2:5-11

What an amazing thing! God's Word contained the exact instructions God had put into my heart. What a confirming moment. What a victory! Satan did not outwit us in this instance.

Approximately three years later the Air Force relocated us about two thousand miles from home. That was far enough away that I felt comfortable sharing with a small group the story of my childhood and the victorious choice that God had directed in my life. The sharing was brief and the words were not dramatic.

The next morning there was a knock on my door, and it

was one of the women who had been at the evening Bible study the night before.

"Are you busy?" she asked. "May I come in for a few minutes?"

"Of course," I replied. She joined me for a cup of tea and then began to explain the reason for her early morning visit.

"It really hit me when you shared about your father last night. In fact, it made such an impact that my husband and I talked about it until well past midnight. You see, my dad is an alcoholic, and last night was the first time I have ever faced that truth and realized how much bitterness I have accumulated in the last twenty-five years."

Her words surprised me. It was impossible not to notice the joy in her eyes and in her heart. God had already begun the forgiving process. It was evident in her words of praise to God.

Forgiveness cannot occur when there is denial of the truth. No matter how ugly the past, or how difficult the situation, God desires for us to be a forgiving people. It is our choice and initially it is a matter of our will.

When we choose to do what is right in God's eyes, when we choose to forgive others for real or imagined wrongs, God begins a supernatural work in us. He will carry our forgiveness beyond our will, to our hearts.

Several years ago, I was speaking to a group of pastors' wives at a retreat. I considered it quite a privilege to provide spiritual nourishment and refreshment for women who stood on the front lines with their husbands. I had come to the conference to minister to them through God's grace. I had no idea how God would minister to me.

My first message was "My Story: Meeting HIM Personally." This is, in part, the story you have just read, about how the Lord saved me and changed my attitude from bitterness to forgiveness. My notes consisted of about five statements on a small sheet of paper. (You don't need extensive notes when you're telling about what God has done in your own life.) The outline was my road map for the message so that I could successfully navigate from the beginning to the end. As I closed the message, we all bowed our heads to pray together. I spoke from my heart about my thankfulness for God's love and for his Word and for the divine appointments we have with him in our lives. Before I knew it, I heard myself say, "And I thank you, Lord, that my father was my father."

I'm certain that the women who were joining me in prayer had no idea of the personal magnitude of what I had just said. Never before had I been able (or even chosen) to say those words. God had honored my act of obedience in forgiving and had gone far "above all that we ask or think" (Ephesians 3:20, KJV). I knew as I spoke those words that God had graciously blessed me with complete forgiveness for my father.

I had a choice. I could have lived with my "if only's" in charge of my life. If only my father had not been an alcoholic. If only he had been healed of this disease before his death. If only I could be sure he had embraced the gospel and received Jesus Christ as his Savior. If only those things had happened, I might have been able to share what God had done in my life. I might have been able to help others see the benefit of forgiveness. If only…

Our attitude is our choice. Choose to forgive.

> When God prepares to do
> something wonderful,
> He begins with a difficulty.
> When he plans to do something
> very wonderful,
> He begins with an impossibility.
> *Author unknown*

3

Choose Jesus

> There is no pit so deep
> that Jesus is not deeper still.
> *Corrie ten Boom*

I had volunteered to work at a Christian book booth at the Illinois State Fair for three days. As I worked, I began to wonder why I had done this. It must have been a weak moment, or maybe I had forgotten what August was like in central Illinois. Working the State Fair was not a prime assignment. The temperature each day was between eighty and ninety-five degrees and the humidity equaled the temperature. The old building that housed the exhibits was not air-conditioned, so at the end of each thirteen-hour day we had to lay the books flat so that their covers would not curl up completely. Each morning we turned the books around again for display.

As I reorganized my book display on the last day of my assignment, someone interrupted my work.

"Kendra?" the woman's voice questioned. "Is that you?"

I turned around to see Amanda, a childhood friend, standing at the edge of the booth. Her family had lived next door to my family when we were growing up. Amanda's younger sister, Jane, had been my very best friend from age four until we left for college. At that time our lives went in two different directions.

As the "older sister," Amanda had had to put up with a lot from us. We were pretty typical younger brats. We faithfully monitored her boyfriends' calls; cast her in all the rotten parts in the plays we wrote, directed, produced, and starred in; bugged her while her friends were visiting her, and so on. You get the picture. She was easygoing and put up with us way beyond what was expected.

Jane and I were not only notorious "little sisters" to Amanda, but for many years we were also inseparable best friends.

> Friendship is the greatest of worldly goods.
> Certainly to me it is the chief happiness of life.
> *C.S. Lewis*

In the summer months Jane and I ate almost every lunch together. Our moms even put up with our eating the main course at one home and the dessert at the other. We'd check the menus at each house, then declare our culinary itinerary.

We walked, biked, and eventually drove to school

together almost every day for twelve years, and had the same teachers from kindergarten through sixth grade. My birthday is on February 22. At the beginning of February when Jane and I were in the first grade, our teacher was giving an overview of the events coming up. There was Valentine's Day, she told us, and the birthdays of two very important people.

"Do any of you know who they are?" asked our teacher.

Someone identified Abraham Lincoln almost immediately, but we all struggled to think of the other important person. Then, suddenly, Jane's hand shot into the air.

"Yes?" asked our teacher.

"Kendra was born in February," Jane said proudly.

The fact that she believed she'd accurately identified a very important person born in February and solved the teacher's riddle gives you a picture of our friendship.

Where Jane was, Kendra was. Where Kendra was, Jane was, and whenever possible we both tagged along with Amanda.

That was thirty years before the August meeting at the book booth on the fairgrounds. Many things had changed over those years.

Amanda went to college first, and three years later Jane and I followed. From that point on our lives did not intersect often. Upon graduating, Amanda worked in Chicago, where she discovered *The Living Bible*, the Moody Bible Institute, and Jesus (in that order). As a young adult I discovered John (my best friend and husband), marriage, and

Jesus. Amanda and I had a new bond, a great bond, that had not existed before. We both loved Jesus. Jane had discovered many things also—but she had not found Jesus.

I dreamed about sharing my faith with my childhood friend. I imagined what I would say to her and how she would respond. Every time I heard the song "Pass It On" I internalized the words in the last verse and thought of Jane.

I wished for Jane the happiness that I'd found. I wanted to shout to her that the Lord of love had come into my life. I'd sing the chorus with great gusto as I thought about Jane.

But I didn't—pass it on, that is. We'd see one another at Christmas and relive our childhood memories. We'd spend time reminiscing and remembering the fun of the past. Amanda and I would keep relatively quiet about our faith. At those holiday reunions we could have talked for hours, maybe even days, about the love we shared for Jesus, but it just wasn't feasible.

That's why the fairground meeting with Amanda was so wonderful! It was a surprise meeting—a splendid serendipity.

"What are you doing here?" I asked Amanda.

"My roommate Barb and I brought her niece, Mindy, to the fair to enter the pigtail contest," Amanda explained.

A glance at Mindy's long braids confirmed that she was definitely a contender.

"I'm here for one more day, selling Christian books," I told her. "Someone relieves me tonight. This is such a treat! Tell me, what's new? How is your job? Your family?" I asked hurriedly. "How are your mom and dad? And Jane and Jay and little Holly?"

"Hold on," Amanda laughed. "One thing at a time. Mom and Dad are doing well."

"You look just like your beautiful mom," I interrupted, suddenly overwhelmed by the similarity and by the subtle passing of time. "And Jane? How is Jane?"

"She's really enjoying being a mom. She's busy and doing pretty well," Amanda answered.

"Does she know Jesus?" I inquired.

"Not yet," Amanda answered, "but with both of us praying, it is just a matter of time."

"What is Jesus doing in your life?" I asked.

Then we began to share our deepest thoughts concerning our love for the Savior.

The next thirty minutes were wonderful. It was the highlight of my State Fair experience. After Amanda finally left the booth that morning, I knew beyond question that this had not been a chance meeting, but that God had blessed me with an encounter *he* had arranged.

> All I have seen teaches me to trust the Creator
> for all I have not seen.
> *Ralph Waldo Emerson*

The next day was even stickier and hotter. It was the saunalike kind of day that appeals only to the corn growing in the fields. It has been said that on steamy August days, if you stand completely still, you can hear the corn grow. Amanda wasn't listening to the corn that day. She and Barb, Barb's mom, sister, and niece were all settled in an air-conditioned car, traveling the Illinois country roads.

Amanda was sitting in the backseat with her roommate's mom as the car navigated the country roads, hemmed in tightly by the gently swaying corn. Country roads are beautiful on a late summer day, but that beauty can be deceptive. The mature corn plants are tall and leafy and can serve as screens blocking intersections—screens that can mask oncoming cars. That is precisely what happened.

As the car carrying my friend Amanda slowed and moved into a blind intersection, an oncoming car from the left could not be avoided. Neither car was able to stop. The next moment had to be one of shock and terror as the two cars collided. The point of impact was the back door of the car. Amanda was killed, and so was Barb's mother.

My phone rang that afternoon after I got home from the fair.

"There was a car accident a few hours ago," said a woman who had grown up in our little town. "Amanda was killed. The officials have already called her sister Jane. I thought you might not know yet."

"I just saw Amanda yesterday," I exclaimed, as though our encounter should somehow have exempted her from harm.

"That's wonderful!" the woman replied. "That might be a comfort to Jane."

The conversation ended, and I immediately dialed Jane's number.

"Jane, I just heard about Amanda. I'm so sorry!" I sobbed. Jane was crying too.

"Jane," I continued, "I just saw Amanda yesterday. We were both at the Illinois State Fair. We spent about half an hour talking together!"

"Oh," Jane cried, "I want you to tell me every word. Jay and Holly and I are on our way home now. It'll take about four hours. Can you meet me at my parents' house?"

"I'll be there when you arrive," I said. "I love you."

As I hung up the phone I turned her words over again and again in my mind. "I want you to tell me every word."

"Lord," I prayed, "help me to remember and recount every word."

> Carry each other's burdens, and in this way
> you will fulfill the law of Christ.
> *Galatians 6:2*

By 3:30 I was waiting in Jane's parents' living room. Moments later Jane arrived. The car pulled up to the house and she rushed inside. Jane and her husband and baby girl were comforted by the many friends who were together. She and I hugged and cried, and finally we stole away to the bedroom to be alone.

"Tell me everything Amanda said," Jane begged. "Tell me your whole conversation."

I had been reconstructing the conversation in my mind for the last four hours, and now I replayed the entire thing as accurately as I could.

"We talked about Amanda's job," I said, "and about your folks. We talked about how sweet your little girl is. We talked about books we'd read, were reading, and wanted to read. And most importantly, we talked about Jesus! In fact," I continued, "that is who we talked about most of the time."

I explained to Jane how important Jesus was to both of us. I told her that he was the most important thing in Amanda's life.

Jane listened intently and constantly encouraged me to continue. When I finally could remember no other piece of conversation I stopped.

Jane looked at me and said quite simply, "I want to be a Christian. Tell me what to do."

God's Word tells us to always be prepared to give an answer to the hope within us (see 1 Peter 3:15). It is for moments like this that we memorize the four spiritual laws. It's moments like this that we imagine as we pray for loved ones.

As coherently as possible, I shared the gospel with Jane. I told her that God loved her and had a wonderful plan for her life. I told her all of us were sinful and that it was this sin that separated us from God. The sin created a huge gulf between God and us. I told her that Jesus was the bridge over this gulf. That he died in our place and rose again. And that he was the only way to God. I told Jane that every person had to receive Christ personally, just as her sister Amanda had done, in order to know God's love.

When I finished the explanation, we prayed together and Jane received Christ as her Savior.

"It's just like the little booklet I read this afternoon," she exclaimed excitedly.

"What?" I asked, completely confused.

"The little booklet. Wait, I'll show you. It's here in my pocket."

Jane reached into her pocket and pulled out a tract. She thrust it into my hands, and I finally understood what she meant.

"Where did you get this?" I asked.

"On our trip home this afternoon we stopped for a cold drink and a restroom break. As I washed my hands, I saw this on the shelf above the sink. I picked it up and glanced at it. I hope it was all right for me to take it, because I did. In the car I read it carefully. Look! It says what you said."

I sat on the bed in shock. All I could do was marvel at the greatness of God. I marveled at his love and his provision. God and one of his obedient ones had prepared Jane's heart hours before I had the privilege of responding to her life-changing statements: "I want to be a Christian" and "Tell me what to do."

Jane had many choices. She could not choose to bring her sister back to life, but she could choose how she would respond to that day's event—the saddest day in her thirty-seven years.

Jane chose Jesus. She chose on that particular day what Amanda had chosen years before. She chose life—eternal life with Christ. She could have chosen bitterness or anger or resentment. She chose just the opposite. She chose the Lord.

Have you made that choice in your life? It doesn't have to be in response to a tragedy like the death of a loved one. If, however, that is the motivation, then let it be, for the important thing is not what brings us to choose Jesus but that we choose Jesus.

> Lord Jesus, I need you. Thank you for dying on the cross for my sins. I open the door of my life and receive you as my Savior and Lord. Thank you for forgiving my sins and giving me eternal life. Take control of the throne of my life. Make me the kind of person you want me to be.
>
> Prayer contained in the
> Campus Crusade for Christ booklet,
> "Four Spiritual Laws"

One hundred years from now
it won't matter if you got that big break,
took the trip to Europe,
or finally traded up to a Mercedes....
It will greatly matter, one hundred years from
now, that you made a commitment
to Jesus Christ.
Author unknown

What good will it be for a man
if he gains the whole world,
yet forfeits his soul?
Matthew 16:26

The highest purpose for faith
is not to change my circumstances
but to change me.
Author unknown

4

Choose to Pray

Pray continually.
1 Thessalonians 5:17

Emily was so sick, so terribly, terribly sick. Her little four-month-old body lay on the sterile white sheets, pale and listless. Her cries were weak and pitiful. There was little indication that anyone should even bother to hope. The physicians had given their edict.

"Emily has an inoperable brain tumor that we suspect is cancerous," they proclaimed. "It's surrounded by blood vessels, making it life-threatening to remove. Any attempt would mean that Emily would surely bleed to death. There is really no hope."

"I don't believe there is no hope," Emily's mother replied. "There is always hope. I've been praying, and so are many others."

It might have been more accurate to say many, many others. Pam and Steve had taken little Emily to their local hospital earlier that morning. Doctors had tested her for a suspected gastrointestinal problem. When the tests showed nothing specific, Emily had been sent home.

After only hours at home, however, Pam knew that Emily needed to go back to the hospital emergency room. Their pediatrician met them there and admitted her for observation. In the night Emily had a seizure and her doctor immediately ordered a CAT scan to be done in the morning. When the scan indicated a mass on the brain, Emily and her family went by ambulance to a larger city and a better-equipped hospital.

It was then that the call went out for others to pray. Pam went through the address book in her purse and tried to think of everyone and anyone who would pray. She knew that prayer could make a difference, so she chose to enlist as many prayer partners as she could.

> Devote yourself to prayer,
> keeping alert in it
> with an attitude of thanksgiving.
> *Colossians 4:2, NAS*

"Of course there's hope," Pam countered. "Emily is still alive. If you won't operate, there must be someone who will."

"Give me until tomorrow," the pediatric neurologist said. "I am having difficulty separating myself from this case emotionally. Perhaps there is some option I can't see at the present time."

"We'll give you the evening to think and we will pray for Emily and for you," Pam replied.

And pray they did! Emily's family and the hundreds of others who knew about her grave situation prayed with fervor.

"That was such a difficult time," Pam admitted. "While we were waiting for the doctor to make suggestions about our next step, it comforted me to envision all the prayer warriors who were hard at work. I imagined them encircling the hospital and holding hands. The group was so large that it went for miles and miles. People whom we had called had called others," she explained. "Prayer concerns have that ripple effect. Those who are praying multiply as the concern is shared with others. Many people who did not even know us prayed for Emily. Hundreds of people, maybe even thousands of people, prayed for her to be healed."

This thought and reading the Word of God comforted Pam. In the Psalms she read, "The Lord is the strength of his people, a fortress of salvation for his anointed one" (Psalm 28:8).

Then Pam had another idea.

"Steve," she declared, "we need to have the elders come from our church and anoint Emily with oil and pray for her healing."

Steve agreed and sent out the request.

> Prayer is an invisible tool
> which is wielded in a visible world.
> *Author unknown*

Meanwhile, as Pam and Steve waited for their church friends to assemble, they were told that if a surgical procedure were attempted, Emily might need blood. The doctors were eager to have her receive healthy blood and concerned about the possible contamination of the existing blood supply. Everyone in the family was tested. Pam and her mother were a perfect match.

"As we prepared to give blood, we had to complete a great deal of paperwork," Pam explained. "At one point, the technician asked for our drivers' licenses. Mom had hers, but I had hurriedly climbed into the ambulance and never imagined I might need it."

"We can't take your blood without the identification of your driver's license," the lab technician explained.

"But I don't have it and my baby is critically ill. She may need my blood," said Pam.

"I doubt if I can take it," the technician replied with an uncaring tone, "but let me make a phone call."

As she left the room to make the call, Pam prayed intently. "Lord, let them take my blood for Emily."

The technician returned and said, "I'm sorry, but there is just no way I can bend the rules. We must have your license."

Just then, an assistant appeared at the door, summoning the lab technician. "I'll be right back," she said as she left the room again.

The exit gave Pam one more opportunity to cry out to God in prayer. "Emily might need my blood, Lord. Please make it possible for me to give it."

Moments later the technician returned looking puzzled and a little chagrined. "That phone call gave me permission to go ahead and take your blood. Believe me, that has never happened before. Roll up your sleeve, please."

Pam smiled with delight. She secretly wondered if perhaps the phone call had come straight from heaven.

By the time Pam and her mom returned to Emily's room, many of their church family had assembled. Although it was a two-hour drive, all of the elders who had been contacted had been able to gather. They circled the hospital crib of little Emily, anointed her with oil, and prayed for her healing.

> I prayed for this child,
> and the Lord has granted me
> what I asked of him.
> *1 Samuel 1:27*

In the morning the pediatric neurologist met with Pam and Steve just as he had promised. He had, in fact, come up with an option. In St. Louis there was a surgeon who was more daring and aggressive than the average doctor. He was also highly skilled.

"It is possible," their doctor explained, "that he will attempt the removal of Emily's tumor, if you are interested."

"We are definitely interested in that option," Pam said. "So what do we do next?"

That question put into motion a plan to try to save Emily's life. Within a few hours, a Life Line plane was ready to take the family to St. Louis. They boarded the plane with Emily, a nurse, and the precious blood that they had miraculously gathered. Perhaps they would need this blood, if surgery were done.

En route and even before the flight, Pam and Steve prayed for guidance in making the right decision. Before they flew to St. Louis, the first neurologist had role-played with them the possible dialog with the surgeon. He let them know the tough presentation they might encounter and the tough call they, as parents, would have to make. Now they could do nothing more than to ask God for guidance.

In St. Louis, they were greeted by a team of specialists who examined Emily and the test records that arrived with her. Finally the consultation began.

"This is definitely a vascular tumor, but I am willing to operate," the surgeon declared. "Her chances of surviving the operation are not good. If she does survive, she runs a high risk of paralysis, blindness, and the very real possibility that the tumor will grow back. We must also consider the fact that the tumor is probably cancerous and that she will have to have chemotherapy and radiation."

The presentation was as harsh as their previous doctor had warned. There was no optimism or glimmer of hope, at least not from the team of physicians.

"So," they asked, "what is your decision?"

"We want you to operate," was the reply.

Undoubtedly the speed of the answer astounded the doctors. It did not surprise Pam and Steve though. They had been praying about what they should do and they felt a peace that passes understanding as they gave their answer.

"What were our other options?" I heard Pam ask, years later. "Really? We wanted to give Emily a chance for life. Our other option was to watch her die. It didn't seem like much of a choice."

That evening after visiting hours were over, a pastor whom Pam and Steve didn't know well came by the hospital.

"I'm sorry I couldn't get here any sooner," apologized Pastor Bob upon his arrival. "We have been praying for you, though. In fact we have felt led to pray specifically that you would have wisdom and discernment. Does that make sense to you?"

It definitely made sense! While the pastor and his prayer team were praying for wisdom and discernment, Emily's parents were making their decision whether or not to allow doctors to operate on the "inoperable" brain tumor.

"God is so amazing," Pam declared. "He had people

praying precisely for our needs. They didn't know us or even know why wisdom and discernment were important."

Later that night, however, Pam felt as if she were wrestling with the devil. Negative thoughts bombarded her mind—thoughts that caused her to question the decision they had made.

"How can you do this to your baby? Why don't you take her home and have as much time as you can have with her? Why do you want to kill her like this?"

> Evening, morning and noon
> I cry out in distress,
> and he hears my voice.
> *Psalm 55:17*

It was a rough night, but God's assurance prevailed. In the morning light, Pam was still certain they had made the right decision.

The doctor scheduled surgery for the next day and informed Pam that Emily would need six pints of blood instead of the two they had transported.

"We'll give more blood," Pam declared. "We can do that."

"I'm sorry, but there isn't enough time to process it adequately," was the reply. "We'll use your two pints first, and then we'll have to use blood from the hospital supply."

Pam felt no peace about that possibility, so she did what

she had done almost continually since the drama began to unfold—she prayed.

"Lord, take care of this problem with the blood. Keep Emily safe from any contaminated blood."

Giving Emily to the surgeon the next day was one of the hardest things Pam and Steve had ever had to do. Early in the morning, the family gathered around her crib, prayed, and sang "God is so good" and "Jesus loves me." Then off she went for a possible six hours of surgery.

"I realized I might never see Emily alive again," Pam said. "The next few hours were tough."

> There is no greater love than the love
> that holds on where there seems
> nothing left to hold on to.
> *G.W.C. Thomas*

In four hours the surgery was complete—and Emily was still alive.

"When we got to the tumor, we discovered that it was not vascular. Well, actually, it had been vascular, but all the vessels going to it had dried up," the doctor explained in amazement.

Pam was ecstatic. This was an almost unbelievable answer to prayer! Emily had survived the surgery! The somber look on the surgeon's face, however, warned Pam there was more to report.

"We got all of the tumor that we could see with the

naked eye," he reported. "I am certain we did not get it all. We sent the mass for a biopsy. Our next step is to wait for the results."

He was done. Those were the facts. But before he left, Pam stopped him. "Oh, by the way," she asked, "how much blood did you use?"

"We used one and a half pints," he replied.

Pam could not contain herself and blurted out, "Isn't that just like God!"

As negative as the doctor had been and as difficult as it was for Emily's family to wait for the biopsy, they still had reason for celebration. They decorated Emily's hospital room with posters saying, "God loves Emily," and, "We love Emily." They taped cards and Scripture verses all over the walls. One special verse was taped to Emily's headboard. It was Jeremiah 29:11: "'For I know the plans I have for you,' declares the Lord, 'plans to prosper you and not to harm you, plans to give you hope and a future.'"

After Emily was back in her room, the anesthesiologist came to check on her. The cheerfulness of the room and the proliferation of Bible verses obviously pleased him.

"I can see that you are Christians," he declared to Emily's family. "I prayed for your baby throughout the surgery."

How amazing! God had answered unspoken prayers. He had provided Emily with a prayer warrior even in the operating room. That was a blessing that had not even been requested.

Look around you and be distressed,
Look within you and be depressed,
Look to Jesus and be at rest.
Author unknown

Within five days, the biopsy report was in. The tumor was definitely malignant, and Emily would have to undergo chemotherapy immediately.

"We don't rate cancer anymore from stage one to stage four," their surgeon explained, "but if we did, this would be off the scale. She will have to have chemotherapy for at least two years in hopes it will prolong her life until she can have radiation."

Another bleak report. But not bleak enough to extinguish Pam's hope. Emily's treatment began the next week. She was on a rigorous schedule of chemotherapy followed by a rest and then chemotherapy again. This regimen was to last for two years. Every three months Emily spent several days in the hospital, undergoing tests. Pam added an important request to her prayer list.

"Each time we went into the hospital," Pam explained, "I asked the Lord to send Emily the perfect roommate. I wanted someone to whom I could witness and for whom I could pray. God answered that prayer time and again."

One of Emily's roommates was a little boy with leukemia. Pam tried to share the encouragement of Christ with this young boy and his family.

"I prayed for openings to lift up Jesus," Pam said. "God's Word is so clear, it says that if we lift him up, he will draw men to himself" (see John 12:32). "I didn't have to do any convincing or coercing, I just had to lift up Jesus."

The little boy's mother knew that Pam prayed for Emily, for her little boy, and for many others, including the doctors and nurses. At one point she told a friend, "Ask Pam to pray for you. She has a hot line to God." She didn't say it maliciously or mockingly; she truly believed that somehow Pam had an inside track to God.

"Her comment gave me the perfect opportunity to tell her that she could have the same access to God through Jesus. God's not finished working in her life yet." And neither is Pam. They are still in contact and get together once a year. Pam's prayer is that one day this woman will establish a relationship with Jesus Christ.

> For I know whom I have believed,
> and am persuaded that He is able
> to keep that which I have committed
> unto Him against that day.
> *2 Timothy 1:12b, KJV*

Chemotherapy continued for the next two years. There were ups and downs and challenges, both physically and emotionally.

"After you've been in a fight like this for an extended length of time," Pam explained, "you begin to feel that you're the Lone Ranger. Other people get on with their lives, but you don't. You have to keep repeating painful scenarios."

At one point Pam was especially drained. The chemotherapy schedule had been a wearying one, and one day she felt that her stamina was gone.

She cried out to God, "Lord, I can go through anything with you, but I want to do something for you. If you could give me someone to witness to, I would be so grateful. You see, I would like to call it quits right now and never take Emily back for chemotherapy again. But if you can give me somebody to whom I can show your love, I know I can go on."

Two days later, it was time once again for Emily's treatment. The clinic was especially crowded that day. After a short while, a young woman came out of one of the treatment rooms. She had a three- or four-year-old in tow and was probably nine months pregnant. As she made her way through the waiting room, she was sobbing.

"When I looked at her, I knew she was the one God wanted me to help," Pam said. "So I grabbed a box of tissues and took them to her and we became the best of friends. In the next year I spent hours with her on the phone."

This new friend asked Pam hard questions. "Why do I have a sick child? How could God do this to my baby?"

"I didn't know the answers to many of her questions. But I told her what I did know: that God loved her and her little boy; and that God was willing to give them both a future and a hope through Jesus," Pam said. "None of us know how long we'll live, but that future and hope will eventually mean a place in heaven. There is no better hope."

God has said, "Never will I leave you;
never will I forsake you."
Hebrews 13:5b

Emily finished chemotherapy, and miraculously the doctors declared that she did *not* need radiation. This was atypical. With Emily's type of cancer these two treatments usually go hand in hand. God had answered another prayer.

I have held many things in my hands
and have lost them all;
But the things I have placed in God's hands,
those I always possess.
Earline Steelburg

Several years have passed now and Emily has had no recurrence of the cancer. She is a beautiful eight-year-old child whose life is a testimony to the amazing power of prayer.

"I don't know why God chose Emily," Pam said tearfully. "I will never know why. I just know that his ways are not our ways."

> "For my thoughts are not your thoughts,
> neither are your ways my ways,"
> declares the Lord.
> *Isaiah 55:8*

Emily, Pam, and the rest of the family volunteer three or four times a year to be houseparents at the Ronald McDonald House. That is where they stayed each time Emily was hospitalized.

"When we are there I tell Emily's story," Pam said. "It's a story of hope and prayer and faith. Some families are obviously receptive and some are not. I gently tell the story to everyone. And if they want prayer, I pray."

Even if they have no desire to pray with Pam, she always asks God to help her focus on one family. She adds that family to her prayer list and encourages them with notes of love for the next few months.

She added Sam to her prayer list. Sam had undergone a stem cell rescue and was suffering from septic shock. His body was greatly damaged. He was on a respirator and the medical prognosis was bleak.

"I had been praying for Sam and his family for months. The next time we visited the Ronald McDonald House, I was able to ask an oncology nurse about his progress," Pam said.

"Pam," she replied, "you don't understand. There can be no progress. He is on a respirator and they are waiting for him to die. There is no hope."

"There is always hope. I believe in miracles," Pam said in response.

"You are not being realistic," the nurse said.

Thus the conversation ended. But Pam's prayers did not. She continued praying for Sam and asking God for a miracle.

The next week Pam's phone rang. It was the oncology nurse.

"Sam just went home," the nurse began. "He has a tracheotomy, but he is off of the respirator. I knew you'd want to know. I can't believe it."

"You will someday," Pam replied. "I know you will someday."

Pam chose to pray. It was a choice. At any point in her journey she could have fallen into the rut of choosing the "if only's." If only Emily had not developed a tumor, Pam might have been a prayer warrior for others. If only Emily had not had to have chemotherapy, Pam might have been able to minister to others. And the list could go on and on. But Pam did not dwell on the "if only's." She chose to pray. We all have that same glorious choice.

A day hemmed with prayer
is less likely to unravel.
Author unknown

Daily prayers will diminish your cares.
Betty Mill

5

Choose Joy

The highest pinnacle
of the spiritual life is not
joy in unbroken sunshine
but absolute and undoubting trust
in the love of God.
W. Thorold

Joy is the holy fire
that keeps our purpose warm
and our intelligence aglow.
Helen Keller

It was Shirley's forty-seventh birthday, a day not unlike other days in Shirley's life. It was filled with activities and events. She had to renew her driver's license, attend a church meeting, and squeeze in jury duty. As Shirley showered to begin her busy day, she felt a lump in her breast. Well, that certainly didn't fit into her schedule. Maybe she'd have time to call her doctor today, *if* she finished her errands soon enough. Later in the afternoon she found the time to call.

"Dr. Clancy?" Shirley inquired. "I hate to bother you, but I figured I should call. When I was showering this morning I felt a lump in my breast."

"It's probably just a clogged milk duct," he reassured her. "Come on in tomorrow and have a mammogram. If it doesn't show anything, we'll wait for a month. If it's still there after that time, give me a call."

This timetable fit Shirley just fine. She went in the next day for the mammogram. It didn't show any abnormalities, so she put the lump out of her mind until several weeks later, after the Christmas holidays. The pesky lump was still there. She called her doctor once again and he scheduled an appointment for a biopsy. As she prepared for the scheduled surgery, a nurse brought in some paperwork.

"We need you to sign this," the nurse told Shirley. "It says that if deemed necessary the physician can do a mastectomy."

"Whew," Shirley exclaimed. "We have now gone from a clogged milk duct to a possible mastectomy. That was incredibly fast!"

As Shirley reached the operating room she questioned the nurses about how long she would be in surgery. Their reply was twenty to forty minutes for a biopsy, two hours for a mastectomy. It was 11:45 A.M. The next thing Shirley was aware of was someone calling her name and trying to rouse her. She opened her eyes. The clock on the wall read

2:00 P.M. Shirley knew the outcome of the surgery.

Things change. Life is not guaranteed in longevity or in quality. Shirley experienced a tremendous change that day. She faced a serious disease—a killer—eyeball to eyeball. Two months before the surgery, Shirley had claimed to be in top condition; now her prognosis was listed as poor. Her health status had changed drastically and officially in a little over two hours. She had no control over her circumstances, but she did have a choice about her attitude.

In the face of this unfolding drama, Shirley could have chosen to play the "what if" game. "What if I never see my kids graduate from high school?" "What if it's even worse than the doctors think?" "What if I can never have a normal day again?" "What if I don't make it until next Christmas?" The "what if" game is a game that has no winner. It is a little like the "if only" exercise.

"If only this hadn't happened to me, I might have been able to do something for Christ. I might have been able to make a difference in someone's life."

"If only I didn't have cancer, I could be joyful."

Shirley could play "what if" or "if only," or she could keep her attitude joyful. The choice was hers to make.

Shirley was scheduled for chemotherapy, and she prepared for it by reading all she could find on the procedure. Each brochure and pamphlet listed possible side effects. "You may experience nausea, fatigue, loss of appetite." And each piece of literature said, "You will experience the loss of your hair."

The use of the verb "may experience" helped Shirley to imagine that she could dodge the majority of the chemotherapy symptoms. But the statement, "You will experience the loss of your hair," really bothered her.

Upon the recommendation of her oncologist Shirley called Jan, a woman who had undergone two mastectomies and who was trained as a counselor for women in similar situations. Shirley told Jan about her difficulty accepting the fact that she would lose her hair.

"I know what you mean," Jan replied. "That was the hardest thing for me, too. It was so terrible."

"Oh, great," Shirley thought, "the last thing I need is someone who is all gloom and doom. Jan said it was terrible. I don't need to hear about terrible."

Then Jan continued. "In fact," she said, "I told my husband I didn't mind putting my boob in the drawer at night but I didn't want to hang my hair on the doorknob."

Shirley laughed out loud. The picture Jan had painted with her words was like a funny cartoon. Jan had given Shirley a tremendous gift that day. She had reminded Shirley that despite the circumstances, she could choose joy and laughter. And that is precisely what Shirley did. Shirley chose to face her situation with joy, and to look for opportunities to laugh and to share joy and laughter with others.

On one of Shirley's visits to her oncologist soon after her surgery, he personally discovered her choice for joy. At that time he informed her that the cancer had not been limited to the breast tissue, but instead it was also located in the lymph nodes. He explained that this created a much more serious problem.

"We do have some good news though," Shirley's doctor stated. "We can give you a drug that will eliminate the estrogen in your body. The estrogen is feeding the cancer."

"What will that mean?" Shirley asked.

"You will immediately enter menopause. You will have hot flashes, become irritable, and the aging process will be accelerated greatly," Shirley's doctor replied.

Shirley looked him straight in the eye and repeated the symptoms: "Immediate menopause. Hot flashes. Irritability and accelerated aging. Please tell me again," she said, smirking. "This is the good news?" Even her doctor had to chuckle as he realized the irony. They determined that good news was definitely a relative matter.

Chemotherapy itself gave Shirley an opportunity to be joyful and to influence others with her attitude. She knew that some women arrived for chemotherapy with no smile, with no makeup, and surrounded by a dark cloud of gloom. She decided to take the opposite approach. For each session she dressed in something bright and cheerful. She made sure her wig (yes, her hair did fall out) was done well, and she wore big, dangly earrings. Equally important was the smile she wore to chemotherapy. Shirley chose joy.

> Consider it pure joy, my brothers,
> whenever you face trials of many kinds.
> *James 1:2*

Several months after Shirley finished chemotherapy, I heard her give a devotional at a convention. Very few people in the audience knew Shirley, and even fewer knew of her circumstances. Her message that day was on the sovereignty of God.

"About twenty years ago I gave a devotional at a women's group. Then I declared, 'Nothing has ever gone wrong in my life because God is in control. He is a sovereign God.' After that message, women in their forties and beyond tried to help me out a little," Shirley explained. "'You're just young. Wait until you have a little more maturity. Wait until you've lived a few more years.' Well," Shirley continued, "today I'm in my late forties and I stand before you to say, 'Nothing has ever gone wrong in my life because God is in control.' He's a sovereign God. That does not mean that Satan is not scheming and making his best attempt to kill, steal, and destroy. But he is the enemy, and I am on the winning side. Nothing bad has ever happened in my life."

Nothing bad, just a radical mastectomy and chemotherapy. Those were merely circumstances, which could affect only Shirley's temporary happiness. She did not allow them to affect her joy.

There's a difference between joy and happiness. Happiness is based on happenings. Joy is an inside job. It's a fruit of the Holy Spirit. Shirley chose joy.

Laughter is a tranquilizer
with no side effects.
Arnold Glasow

"You know you're in trouble when the 'best if used by' date on your donors' card has expired," Shirley quipped and then laughed enthusiastically as though she just heard that joke for the first time.

I laughed, too, because it was funny and she was funny. I'm always refreshed in her presence.

Several years ago, Shirley and I were attending a surprisingly somber and boring conference when to our amazement we found ourselves plotting a mutiny—a takeover of the stage, the microphone, and ultimately (hopefully) the mood of the conference. We found three other willing participants and developed our plan.

Right at the point when the emcee dismissed the group for morning break, we cued the sound man to begin our tape. The Amy Grant recording blared out "Fat Baby," at which point we emerged from behind the curtain as Amy, backup singers (Wah,Wah,Wah), and two grown men dressed in shorts, T-shirts, and dorm bed sheet diapers.

The plan went off without a hitch. The audience went wild. The laughter was uproarious. And the great success of the stunt somehow even landed us in the good graces of the conference leaders. I guess they needed a good laugh too.

What a risk we took, all for joy and laughter. Emerson once said, "Laugh often, laugh much." Shirley knew the power of laughter in those relatively carefree years and she knew its power now, when calamity could have been king.

Shirley is not alone in the realization of the power of laughter and joy. The most influential catalyst thrusting laughter to a place of prominence as a positive influence on people and their health was probably Norman Cousins. Cousins prescribed laughter for himself. "He got relief from pain from a degenerative disease when he guffawed his way through humorous videos."[1]

Today researchers can explain the positive effects of laughter and a joyful outlook. "After you laugh, you go into a relaxed state," explains John Morreall, Ph.D., president of HUMORWORKS Seminars in Tampa, Florida. "Your blood pressure and heart rate drop below normal, so you feel profoundly relaxed. Laughter also indirectly stimulates endorphins, the brain's natural painkillers."[2] A Loma Linda University study showed that "thirty minutes after twenty medical students laughed through a video of a well-known comedian, their disease-fighting white blood cells increased by 25 percent."[3]

Norman Cousins had to leave the hospital to view the humorous, health-enhancing videos. Now it is possible to receive a dose of laughter without checking out of the hospital. There are now hospitals with clown schools on site, humor carts, and imported clowns.[4]

The truth of the positive power of choosing joy and

laughter is not new. God's Word is filled with statements verifying the fact:

- A cheerful heart is good medicine (Proverbs 17:22a).
- A happy heart makes the face cheerful (Proverbs 15:13a).
- A cheerful look brings joy to the heart.... The cheerful heart has a continual feast (Proverbs 15:30a; 15:15b).
- The joy of the Lord is your strength (Nehemiah 8:10b).

Why, it has even been suggested that God has a sense of humor. Think of the duckbilled platypus and the aardvark, two of God's more humorous creations. Consider God's plagues against the Egyptians. They were ingenious and some were almost funny. Envision Jesus talking about taking the speck out of your brother's eye while there is a log in yours. That's a funny picture.[5]

All of this adds up to a great deal of support for the choice of joy. And yet sometimes we fail to choose joy. What can keep us from this choice? What things did Shirley have to combat in order to choose joy?

She told me once that besides Satan, whose number one mission, as we read in John 10:10a, is to steal, kill, and destroy, there are other potential robbers of joy. The general attitude of society is one great big joy-robber. Think about it. The evening news is usually pretty depressing. The world, it would seem, is going to hell in a handbasket. Any evening, in just thirty minutes you can relive murders, robberies, social injustices, blight, and numerous natural disasters. Pretty depressing, huh?

Then there's the weather. Tomorrow we have a 10 percent chance of rain. (Oh, no! My cookout will be ruined.) Wait a minute! A 10 percent chance of rain means a 90 percent chance of sunshine. (I won't cancel the cookout after all.) The negative attitude of our society can rob us of our joy.

Stress is another deterrent to joy. We used to think of young business executives as the only ones living stressful lives. Now we hear that stress is a leading negative in the lives of teenagers.

Shirley once gave me a copy of a stress diet that she had discovered. Here it is:

Stress Diet

BREAKFAST:

1/2 grapefruit

1 slice whole wheat bread

8 oz. skim milk

LUNCH:

4 oz. lean broiled chicken

1 c. steamed zucchini

1 Oreo cookie

Herb tea

AFTERNOON SNACK:
Remainder of Oreo package
1 qt. Rocky Road ice cream
1 jar hot fudge

DINNER:
2 loaves garlic bread
Large pepperoni pizza
2 Milky Way candy bars
Whole frozen cheesecake,
eaten directly from freezer

Helpful Hints:

- If no one sees you eat it, it has no calories.
- If you drink a diet soda with a candy bar, they cancel each other out.
- When eating with someone else, there is no need to count calories if you both eat the same amount.
- Food taken for medicinal purposes, such as hot chocolate, toast, and Sara Lee Cheesecake, never counts.
- If you fatten up those around you, you will look thinner.

I'm not sure that the diet relieved my stress, but the laughter it evoked made a difference.

Negative people can also rob us of our joy. Attitudes are contagious. When Shirley's white count was down after chemotherapy, she avoided people with colds and the flu. Regardless of her blood count status, however, she avoided people with negative attitudes.

Shirley told me once that fear was another joy-robber. One weekend about six months after her cancer was discovered, Shirley started vomiting. Ultimately she was so dehydrated that her husband had to take her to the emergency room of a local hospital. After the attending physician examined her and asked her many questions about the medications she had been taking, he asked her a question followed by a statement that instantly produced fear in Shirley's mind.

"Have you had a brain scan recently?" the emergency doctor inquired. "I think the cancer has gone to your brain."

Shirley reacted not only with fear but also with anger: "I'm going to let my oncologist do all the diagnosing of cancer. Thank you very much."

The doctor didn't press his diagnosis, but his guess had done its temporary damage. Shirley told me that from the moment of his careless statement until the next Tuesday, when she could finally visit her oncologist, she was plagued with fear. The visit on Tuesday with her cancer doctor was very positive. She did not have a brain tumor. It was then that Shirley realized that fear had successfully stolen her joy for several days.

"Do you know what fear is?" Shirley asked me once. "It is:

F — alse

E — vidence

A — ppearing

R — eal

When we realize that, we've stripped fear of its power." That definition went a long way toward restoring Shirley's joy.

I remember Shirley telling me about a get-together for a friend before his surgery. It was estimated that he had a 5 percent chance. As the evening and the party unfolded, Shirley realized she really didn't know too much about the circumstances of the illness, the surgery, or the 5 percent chance. She decided that there was no time like the present to ask some questions.

"So you're scheduled for surgery on Thursday, right?" Shirley asked the upcoming patient.

"That's right," he replied.

"I hear you have a 5 percent chance. What exactly does that mean?"

"The doctor says I have a 5 percent chance of having a heart attack in recovery from my gall bladder surgery," he said gloomily.

"A 5 percent chance of a heart attack?" Shirley howled. "That means a 95 percent chance of no heart attack. Those are terrific odds!"

The man paused and then seemed to understand the

math for the very first time. A smile came across his face, followed by a smirk, and then a belly laugh. Before long the other guests were wondering what could possibly be so amusing that Shirley and the guest of honor were laughing to the point of tears.

> Laughter is the sun that drives winter
> from the human face.
> *Author unknown*

From the outset, Shirley's prognosis was listed on her medical records as poor. After five years of joyfully fighting the disease and testing cancer-free, Shirley asked her physician if he could upgrade her prognosis. On her prodding, he finally changed the record from "prognosis—poor" to "prognosis—guarded."

"This is an upgrade?" she asked jokingly. And then she accepted her victory, be it ever so small.

I have heard people say that at best life is terminal. That is true. After seven and a half years, Shirley faced two more rounds of chemotherapy, one round of radiation, and many doses of powerful medication. As we ate lunch together one day, after all these medical procedures, I asked Shirley if she ever asked the physicians what her life expectancy was.

"I don't bother to ask the doctors," she replied. "What do they know for sure? Besides, I just signed the paperwork for a fifteen-year mortgage on our new house."

Later that day I heard her tell the story of the two sisters who faithfully ate oat bran and lived long and healthy lives. Ultimately these two women died and went to be with Jesus in glory. One sister was practically speechless over the beauty and awesomeness of heaven. The other sister seemed to be pouting. When the first sister finally realized that she was alone in her excitement, she asked the pouting sister why.

"Well," said the sober sister, "if you hadn't made me eat all that oat bran, I could have been here sooner."

Shirley laughed, actually before the punch line, and I laughed too. It was funny, Shirley was funny, and her joy was contagious.

> Until further notice, celebrate everything.
>
> *Author unknown*

A joyful person, one choosing joy in spite of the circumstances, is one who celebrates life and embraces the abundant life. So on that day, Shirley and I ate lunch together and celebrated our friendship. We celebrated life and its fragility. We celebrated joy. And we celebrated the sovereignty of God. Shirley has chosen joy.

> The most wasted of all our days are those in which we have not laughed.
>
> *Sebastian Chamfort*

6

Choose Not to Worry

Worry is a darkroom
where negatives are developed.
Author unknown

Cast all your anxiety on him
because he cares for you.
1 Peter 5:7

Betty didn't get smacked around every day; just often enough to keep her jumpy. The frequency of Pete's hitting her was unpredictable.

"There was nothing I could do to avoid provoking Pete," she said. "There was no logic, no formula. What made him mad one day didn't bother him the next. Something that didn't faze him today might send him into a rage tomorrow."

It took Betty many years to realize that her husband's explosions could not be eliminated by anything she did or didn't do. The unpredictability of his angry attacks kept her off balance and kept Pete in control of her life.

"He would throw me against the wall, or down the stairs, or into furniture when he was angry," Betty explained. "And he would swing at me, connecting with my face most of the time. I remember wishing he'd break my jaw, so that I would have to go to the doctor."

At the same time that she wanted to see a doctor, she was also reluctant to see one. Part of the ploy of an abusive husband is to convince his wife that the abuse is *her* fault. He leads her to believe that she has caused the lashing out and that she has done something to "deserve" the beatings. This makes it very difficult for the woman to seek help, lest her helpers tell her she's to blame.

Logic and sound thinking tell us that this line of reasoning is absurd. What could anyone do to "deserve" being hit by another person? Logic, however, is not part of an abusive relationship.

"We had a very unreliable car, and it invariably acted up when I had it on the road," Betty said. "One day, I had stopped at the grocery store and it refused to start. I cranked the ignition key and tried every trick I could think of to get it started. Finally, I had no choice except to call Pete. He arrived and fiddled under the hood until the car started. Then I followed him home."

The scene that followed was terrifying. When she drove up, Pete pulled her from the car and shoved her into the garage.

"Why couldn't you get the *^&*^% car started?" he shrieked. "You are so *^%$^ stupid! I'm going to beat some sense into you so that this doesn't happen again."

He pushed and struck her, but quickly got bored with the one-sided fight. In frustration he walked to his truck and roared out of the driveway.

Betty lay crumpled in a back corner of the garage. The blows Pete had landed had not been as bad as usual, but Betty's spirit was broken. She thought long and hard about the possibility that Pete might one day kill her during one of these beatings. It was a thought she had lived with for several years. Who would care for their children if she were gone?

Twelve years before, when this young couple had been dating, Betty hadn't noticed any short-fuse or abusive behavior in Pete. Maybe she had been blinded by infatuation, or by Pete's dashing good looks. Her parents had had some reservations about him, but they had been reassured when Betty told them that Pete had said he was a Christian.

"My mistake was listening to his talk and not watching his walk," she said, years later. "I heard what I wanted to hear, and I hid my eyes from the signs that he was lying when he said he was a Christian."

After they were married, Betty discovered that Pete had no desire to be involved in a church, and he had no intention of worshiping with her on Sunday morning. In fact he attempted to sabotage Betty's efforts to attend church.

"Pete wanted to go the bars and to party on Saturday night. He would get angry with me when I went along because I didn't want to drink," Betty explained. "And he'd get just as angry if I stayed home. He absolutely refused to get up for church the next morning, and he did everything he could to get me to stay home, too."

It did not take long for Betty to realize that Pete had married her under false pretenses. Pete was not a Christian. In fact, he seemed to loathe the church and people who had accepted Christ.

"At first I worried a great deal about his salvation," Betty said. "What could I do to bring him to Christ? What could I say?"

But the more Betty attempted to say and do the perfect thing to lead Pete to a saving knowledge of Christ, the more Pete seemed to reject the Lord.

"At one point, I realized that my worry was not accomplishing a thing. I could not worry Pete into heaven, nor could I push him in. My responsibility was to live in a Christlike manner before him. So," she continued, "I chose to give him to God. I had to quit worrying."

> Don't worry about anything; instead pray about everything; tell God your needs and don't forget to thank him for his answers. If you do this you will experience God's peace, which is far more wonderful than the human mind can understand.
>
> *Philippians 4:6-7, TLB*

Although Betty finally chose to stop worrying about Pete's relationship with Christ (or lack of it), she was rapidly making other disturbing discoveries about her new husband.

"Within months of our wedding, I became pregnant. I couldn't believe it and was momentarily taken aback. 'We're already off to a rocky start,' I thought. 'How will I handle this added responsibility?'"

She discovered all too soon how Pete would react to his new and increased responsibility. It was when she was pregnant with Jessica, their older daughter, that Pete first became violent. He came home late one night after spending the evening in the bars. Betty wondered where he had been and she met him at the door.

"I'm so glad you're home," she said. "Did you have car trouble?"

"No, I didn't have *any* trouble," Pete said angrily. "And it's none of your business if I did. I don't need to report in to you all the time. You're not my mother!"

With that he struck her in the face with the back of his hand and marched into the house. The blow caused Betty to stumble backward. Her cheek was stinging, and her heart was broken.

How could her husband hit her? What if she had tripped and fallen? What if the baby had been hurt? The incident left her questioning what her future was to be.

By morning, Betty had made a decision. She could not live with a man who hit her. And she could not bring a new baby into a violent household. She packed up her essentials and left Pete, returning to her parents' home in a nearby community.

Pete did not realize what had happened until he came home from work late that afternoon. When he discovered Betty was gone, he made a quick phone call to her parents' home.

"Is Betty there?" he asked.

"She is," her dad replied, "but she is not interested in speaking to you."

"What's going on? I don't understand. If it's about last night, well, I can explain that. I had a little too much to drink and when Betty met me at the door, she startled me. I didn't mean to hurt her. I would never hurt her. I am so sorry. Please forgive me," he pleaded. "Nothing like this will ever happen again. Please, please let me talk to Betty and tell her how sorry I am." They talked, and Betty went home.

Saying "I'm sorry" is so easy. Meaning it and having a repentant heart and a change in behavior are much more difficult. Pete's "I'm sorry" was meaningless, as Betty would soon discover.

After little Jessica was born, the abusive behavior surfaced again. With a baby in the house, Betty thought that it might be nice to have a second car. Pete wasn't always easy to catch at work, and she hated having to depend on a neighbor if Jessica needed to go to the doctor. It would also be nice to grocery shop during the day, she thought, instead of waiting until Pete got home in the evening.

A young man Betty and Pete knew had a car with a For Sale sign on it. Betty suggested they drive over and take a look at it. The battle didn't begin until after they returned home.

"Did you like the car?" Betty asked.

"I thought it was overpriced," Pete replied.

"Oh, I don't know," continued Betty. "He said it had four new tires and had recently had a tuneup."

"I don't know why you should trust him," Pete growled back. "Do you think he knows more about cars than I do?"

"I didn't say that," Betty replied. "I just thought it was a nice car."

"I don't *care* what you think," Pete yelled. By now he was visibly angry. "You don't know anything, anyway!"

"Fine, let's just drop it," Betty suggested. "We don't need to get that car."

"No, I'm not going to drop it! If you think you know more about cars than I do, you can just get out of here and get *yourself* a car," Pete exploded.

By now there was no turning Pete's anger back, and nothing that Betty could say or do would soothe him. He reached across the table and grabbed her arm. Even though she yelled at him to stop, he jerked her out of the chair and literally dragged her across the kitchen floor. When he got to the back door, he opened it and pushed her into the yard with all his strength. Betty lay in the backyard, sobbing and struggling to grasp what had happened.

This time Betty did not go to her parents' home. In her confused state of mind she thought she had used up her second chances. Now she would have to stick it out and make the best of the situation. And unbeknownst to Pete or to her folks, Betty was pregnant again.

> The Lord shall preserve thy going out
> and thy coming in from this time forth,
> and even for evermore.
> *Psalm 121:8, KJV*

Those of us in healthy marriages have a difficult time understanding what holds a woman in an abusive relationship such as Betty's. We don't understand the *despair* that binds a woman's hands against action. The abuser convinces his spouse that there is no hope and that no one can help her. The result is unremitting despair.

Guilt is another binding force. The victim is brainwashed into believing that *she* is responsible for the abuser's violent actions.

Pride can also hold an abused woman in a frightening situation. She does not want to admit that she has chosen a mate so poorly.

Fear and *worry* about life, limb, family, and future also trap the abused woman. How will she survive financially?

Betty was a Christian, and she felt certain that with God's help she would be able to restore the marriage. She didn't think that divorce was an option.

> I will lift up my eyes to the mountains;
> from whence shall my help come?
> My help comes from the Lord,
> who made the heaven and earth.
> *Psalm 121:1-2, NAS*

With the arrival of their second child, Sally, Betty became more concerned about the lack of parenting the girls received from Pete. Typically he ignored them or acted as though they were a nuisance. He provided no spiritual guidance or encouragement to them.

"I remember lying in my bed one night and realizing Pete was not going to be the father that he was supposed to be to the kids. I knew that, and I knew I had to go forward and do what I could to be a good mother to my children. I wanted them to have a Christian home and a church. I realized that in the spiritual sense, I was responsible for these young lives. I needed to teach them the ways of the Lord and bring them the gospel. That was my responsibility. I also had to understand that I was not responsible for my husband's salvation or his parenting. I said to God, 'I'll be their mother, but you're going to have to be their father. They don't have a father who will pray with them or read the Bible to them or teach them about you. You are going to have to father them. I'm not going to worry. I know you will meet their needs.'"

Betty relinquished this worry and responsibility to God. She was not going to be able to control Pete's interaction with the girls by worrying.

> Therefore do not worry about tomorrow, for tomorrow will worry about itself. Each day has enough trouble of its own.
>
> *Matthew 6:34*

While Betty tried not to worry about Pete's salvation or poor parenting skills, she was worried that someday in a fit of rage Pete might take her life. If that ever happened, who would care for her children?

One day things came to a frightening head for Betty. It had been an exhaustingly combative day. It seemed as though Pete had reacted negatively to every word she had spoken. Even the dinner she served made him angry. It looked as though another explosion was imminent.

Betty was on pins and needles all day. Somehow she was able to avoid any form of conflict throughout the day, but by nightfall she was exhausted. It was all she could do to finish the dishes, help the kids with their homework, and fall into bed. She had avoided physical attack, but she was exhausted by the verbal attacks Pete had volleyed at her all day.

"Dear Lord," she prayed, "I don't know how much more I can take. Please, Father, do something. I can't go on much longer."

And the still small voice of God spoke to her heart: "It won't be much longer now."

Betty knew in that instant that God was going to take care of her. She interpreted God's words to mean that her time on earth would be ending before too long. She felt that God was telling her that he had things under control.

Yes, God did have everything under control, but Betty's life on earth was not coming to an end. Instead, her torturous living conditions were soon to change. That night Betty chose not to worry about her own life. She put her trust wholly in God.

> Do not be anxious about anything, but in everything, by prayer and petition, with thanksgiving, present your requests to God.
>
> *Philippians 4:6*

Within two weeks Betty's nephew confronted her about the abuse he suspected. When she admitted the severity of her situation, her nephew encouraged her to leave Pete. She left her children with a friend and boarded a plane bound for her parents' new home in another state. In this protective setting, Betty took time to sort through the facts and her feelings. The time away was like a sweet balm. She was able to clear her head and see the futility of continuing in her dangerous living situation. From that time on, she never again lived with Pete.

Studies show that an abused woman's safety is most at stake after she leaves her abuser. That fact alone could have caused Betty to worry. And what about a place to live? Her family was not living in Betty's hometown, and she wanted to keep the girls in their own school. She wanted to keep their lives as normal as possible.

Betty chose not to worry. She had a restraining order put on Pete and tried to be wise about having friends from church escort her and the girls to their school activities. Her church also rose to the occasion and helped her find housing—first in a friend's extra room, and then in low-income housing. Somehow, miraculously, the Lord met Betty's financial needs.

"One day when we came home to the apartment," she said, "we found an envelope had been slipped under the door. It contained seven one-hundred-dollar bills. That was it! No name, no address, no one to thank but God."

Betty chose not to worry but to let God meet their needs. By this time, she had been practicing not worrying with regularity, and it was becoming easier and easier to make a positive choice.

> Worry never robs tomorrow of its sorrow,
> it only saps today of its joy.
> *Leo Buscaglia*

Many of us worry about things that are much less monumental than those Betty had in her life. It's not that we like to worry or that we need to worry. More than anything, worry is a habit.

"It's only natural to worry," you say. "After all, Kendra, I come from a rich heritage of worriers. My mother worried, my grandmother worried, and her mother before her. It's genetic. All the women in my family worry."

Nice try, but I really don't think worry is genetic. I think it's a choice. The problem is that we have been trained and conditioned to worry, and worrying has become our natural response to many situations.

I was eating dinner one day with a large group of friends. Something was obviously bothering the young woman sitting next to me. As we were being served dessert, she finally addressed the issue that had been on her mind.

"Kendra, I want to talk to you about something," she began.

"Sure," I replied, and encouraged her to go on.

"I am worried about something," she continued. "I am worried about my kids."

I did a quick mental inventory and realized there was seemingly nothing to worry about when it came to her kids. She had two healthy, happy boys who were well-behaved and achieving well in school.

"Have I missed something?" I asked. "Is there something wrong with one of the boys? Is there a problem at school or at home?"

"Well," she hesitated, "no, there isn't anything in particular. I just worry about them."

"Let me reassure you that you have great kids and there is no need to worry," I said.

"There's something else. I worry about my husband," she said sheepishly.

Again I racked my brain to see if I could identify what might be motivating this particular worry. Again I came up blank.

"Why are you worrying about your husband? He's healthy. He loves you and is a good father and provider. Do you really have any reason to worry about him?" I asked.

"No, I guess not," she sighed. "Oh, I also worry about plane crashes."

"Do you have any airplane tickets? Do you know anyone who has ever been in a plane crash?" I questioned as patiently as possible.

"No," she said with a hint of embarrassment. "But, Kendra, there is one more thing."

"Sure, go ahead," I said, wondering where we were going from here.

"I worry that maybe I worry too much," she blurted out.

"Now, I just might agree with you on that one," I said, laughing.

Blessed is the man who is
too busy to worry in the daytime
and too sleepy to worry at night.
Author unknown

Worry can be consuming. I once heard it said that worry time is wasted time. So it would seem that choosing *not* to worry is a positive choice. How can we do it?

I learned an important lesson long ago at a Little League park. All three of my boys played Little League baseball. When our eldest son was about ten years old, he went into the game one night as a relief pitcher. Now, just in case some of you are unfamiliar with Little League, let me help you out. These are little boys, eight, nine, and ten years old. The role of the pitcher is paramount because it is very seldom that one of the boys hits the ball. If the pitcher pitches strikes, the batters typically strike out. If he pitches balls, the bases fill up mighty quick. You see, runs are scored not so much by making hits but by loading the bases with walks.

On this particular night, the bases were downright crowded when Matthew went in to pitch. You can imagine the kind of night the previous pitcher had had, to load up the bases. Matthew took his spot on the mound, wound up, and threw the ball.

“Ball one,” the umpire shouted.

My motherly instincts and my overwhelming urge to

help overtook my brain and I yelled some constructive words to Matthew.

"Pitch a strike, Matthew," I bellowed from the stands.

The wind up … the pitch …

"Ball two," the umpire countered.

It was obvious to me that Matthew had not heard me. So this time I yelled even louder.

"PITCH A STRIKE, Matthew," I cried.

"Ball three," said the umpire.

Maybe if I said it slower it would help.

"P-I-T-C-H A S-T-R-I-K-E, Matthew," I howled.

To tell you the honest truth, I don't remember if that next pitch was a ball or a strike. I vaguely recall that Matthew did provide relief and his team won the game. I do vividly remember, however, our conversation after the game.

"Mom," Matthew began, "I really don't mind if you cheer at ballgames. (What a relief! I am a cheerfully vocal fan.) But please don't ever yell, 'Pitch a strike.' Because you see, Mom, if there is anyone in the whole ball field who wants to pitch a strike, it is me! I understand the goal."

Now, I am not a slow learner. I got his message, and his brothers after him benefited greatly from the lesson I learned that evening. So I won't tell you—

"Stop worrying!!"

"STOP WORRYING!!"

"S-T-O-P W-O-R-R-Y-I-N-G!!" You probably already want to do that. Instead, let's see if I can give you some suggestions to help you stop worrying.

One of the truths that has helped me is to realize that *worry consumes priceless, irreplaceable energy.* Typically, my worry list pops into view after I've fallen asleep for the night. Maybe I'm unique in this, but more times than not, I can make it through the day just fine with no time spent in worry. Then give me three or four hours of good sleep and my brain seems to suddenly turn back on and focus in on a list of worries. This list may contain significant issues or extremely trivial ones, but either way it wakes me up and keeps me awake for varying amounts of time. In the morning, the issues—big or small—are still there, and I am exhausted. Worry has accomplished nothing except to rob me of precious rest. Don't waste energy in worry.

Another key to help you "pitch a strike" and stop worrying is to remember that *worry is a lack of faith.* "Therefore I tell you, do not worry about your life, what you will eat or drink; or about your body, what you will wear. Is not life more important than food, and the body more important than clothes? Look at the birds of the air; they do not sow or reap or store away in barns, and yet your heavenly Father feeds them. Are you not much more valuable than they? Who of you by worrying can add a single hour to his life?" (Matthew 6:25-27). Either we believe God is in control or we do not.

This leads me to my third suggestion. Why do we think that life would be better if *we* were in control? We worry that things won't go the way we planned. But who says our plans are the best? We worry when we are unable to move all the chess pieces of life to the squares we have chosen for them. In order to stop worrying, *we must release control of our lives to God*.

Finally, let me present an age-old remedy for worry. It is called preparation. How many times do we worry about the things that we have failed to prepare for? Ask any student who has failed to study if he is worried. *Preparation can replace worry.*

> Worry is like a rocking chair:
> It gives you something to do,
> but doesn't get you anywhere.
> *Author unknown*

Several months ago I had a Pap test with worrisome results. I went to my physician and he recommended that I visit a specialist. I was able to get an appointment within two weeks and met with my new doctor.

"I don't recommend that you have another Pap test," she said. "Instead, I suggest that you have a biopsy. We'll take some tissue from your cervix and send it to the lab, and that will give us a much better idea of what we are dealing with."

Since I do not have a medical degree and her recommendation seemed wise, I had the biopsy that same morning. Many women reading this book know the uneasy feeling you have while waiting for the results of a biopsy. For those of you who have never personally experienced this, trust me when I tell you that worrying appears to be one of the most plausible options (and probably one of the most widely selected).

"When will my results be in?" I asked.

"It may take up to two weeks," the assistant replied.

I kept thinking that surely in this age of men on the moon, E-mail, and instant mashed potatoes, they could find out about my health a little sooner. But I held my tongue and said that I would be waiting to hear from them. Then I drove home, worrying just a little.

The medical procedure I had just experienced was not a very big deal. "A little uncomfortable," I believe was how the doctor described it, but definitely not a major procedure.

When I got home I was mildly sick to my stomach so I went up to the bedroom to lie down. Unfortunately, I was not tired, and after twenty minutes of staring at the ceiling fan, I decided maybe I could accomplish some work while lying in a horizontal position. I also realized that working would give me something else to worry—oops!—think about besides my health.

My laptop computer was close by, and I propped up my back and head and put the computer, case and all, on my stomach. As I unzipped the case, a greeting card fell out of the pocket. It was a card I had purchased weeks before to put in my card stash—a collection of cards waiting to be mailed at the appropriate time to the appropriate person. I was astonished as I looked at the card.

On the front was a cartoon picture of a skier with great big eyes going off an obviously unexpected jump. The caption read, “Be anxious for nothing ...” Inside it read: “God is still in control!” In a way, I had sent myself a greeting card. Unless you have a *really bad* memory, that doesn’t happen too often.

I smiled and marveled at the goodness of God’s provision. I needed the reminder and he knew it! Even though I knew Betty’s story and I’d seen her peace and lack of worry firsthand, I needed to be reminded. *Choose not to worry, Kendra.*

I am thankful for the reminder, and I am thankful that on that day I was able to make the choice not to worry, even before the biopsy results—showing no cancer—were in. I am also thankful that God has given me an example like Betty. She is a woman whose life circumstances were fertile ground for worry, and yet with God’s help she has chosen *not* to worry. I’ve never heard her say, “If only Pete hadn’t hit me ... If only our two daughters had a decent father ... If only Pete hadn’t lied about being a Christian....”

Through Betty’s life and story God reminds me not to worry. His love letter, the Bible, is filled with reminders not to worry. God encourages all of us, regardless of our situation, to choose not to worry.

So do not fear, for I am with you;
do not be dismayed, for I am your God.
I will strengthen you and help you;
I will uphold you with my righteous right hand.
Isaiah 41:10

Give your troubles to God;
He will be up all night anyway.
Author unknown

7

Choose to Be Content

> Jealousy is the tribute
> mediocrity pays to achievers.
> *Author unknown*

Joan wandered down the hall to the small waiting room attached to the newborns' nursery. She felt remarkably perky, considering that she had given birth to a baby girl just hours before. The labor had been easy and delivery had been very quick. Baby Elizabeth's APGAR score (a test that measures the responses of a newborn) was a healthy eight, and the infant had nursed eagerly in the birthing room. After a while nurses had taken Elizabeth to the nursery to clean her up, Joan's husband, Greg, had gone to the pay phone to notify relatives, and Joan had closed her eyes to rest.

Now, an hour or so later, Joan, refreshed and ready to spend more time with her little girl, wandered down to the nursery and entered the small waiting room attached to the babies' room.

The door to the babies' room was ajar, and as Joan relaxed in a rocker, waiting for a nurse to emerge, she heard bits and snatches of conversation—just isolated words and pieces of dialogue. "Mom sick?" "Rubella?" "Retarded ..." "Head size..." "Handicapped..."

"I knew they were talking about Elizabeth and my heart began to break into a million pieces." Joan told me years later as she related the facts of that day. "They never mentioned my name or Greg's or Elizabeth's, but I knew that the concerned conversation was about us. Moments later Greg joined me, and as we both heard more sentence fragments, our concern grew. Finally, a doctor came out of the nursery door and saw us sitting in the room adjacent to the nursery. He had no idea how long we had been sitting there."

He began to speak, but Joan interrupted him."We have a problem, don't we?" Joan questioned. The doctor nodded his head.

> Motherhood is partnership with God.
>
> *Author unknown*

Joan had been teaching school while pregnant. In her sixth month, she contracted a virus—cytomegalovirus. This virus rarely causes serious disease in healthy people, but when an expectant mother becomes infected during pregnancy, the infant is at risk for congenital infection. The virus was probably carried to her classroom by one of her students, who may not have even appeared ill. Joan, however, contracted the virus and became very sick. She sensed at that time that things were not right with her pregnancy.

"I am not a worrier," Joan told Greg one day. "You know that. It's just that I can't seem to shake the feeling that something is wrong."

Greg had no particular answers to his wife's concerns. He always comforted and reassured her that God had everything under control.

Late one night Joan was lying awake in bed. As she lay there, she began to pray—to talk to God about all the things that were on her mind. As she scrolled through the day's events and the joys and challenges they had brought, she realized that her greatest concern was for her unborn baby. She was concerned the baby had been affected somehow by her illness.

"Lord, you know the concern of my heart. It is not a fear that something is wrong, but rather a strong feeling. It's almost like a message from you, but I'm not sure. Is that what it is? Are you telling me something about our little baby? Was the baby hurt by my illness?" Joan honestly questioned the Lord, but how could she know the answer? She asked, "If my concern is warranted, God, please have the baby kick."

Although mother and child had been lying completely still for hours, at the precise moment of Joan's statement, the unborn child kicked with great force. It was such a hard kick that Joan could not ignore it or pretend it hadn't happened. But still she questioned whether it was God responding to her prayer or whether it was her own imagination.

Joan pondered the midnight conversation with the Lord for several days. She became more and more convinced the baby's kick had been no coincidence. Instead she decided it must have been from God. Joan decided to mimic the fleeces of Gideon.

"Gideon said to God, 'If you will save Israel by my hand as you have promised—look, I will place a wool fleece on the threshing floor. If there is dew only on the fleece and all the ground is dry, then I will know that you will save Israel by my hand, as you said.' And that is what happened. Gideon rose early the next day; he squeezed the fleece and wrung out the dew—a bowlful of water.

"Then Gideon said to God, 'Do not be angry with me. Let me make just one more request. Allow me one more test with the fleece. This time make the fleece dry and the ground covered with dew.' That night God did so. Only the fleece was dry; all the ground was covered with dew" (Judges 6:36-40).

"God, if there is something wrong with this baby," Joan said, "do not allow him or her to kick any more until birth."

And that is precisely what happened. The child did not kick again before birth.

> As a mother, my job is to take care of the possible and trust God with the impossible.
> *Ruth Bell Graham*

Now, sitting in the nursery of the hospital, Joan looked up at the physician and asked, "We have a problem, don't we?" already knowing the answer in her heart.

"We have a very serious problem," he answered. "Your little girl is severely mentally retarded."

Little Elizabeth was just hours old. Her parents, who should have been experiencing great joy at her birth, were instead experiencing grief. She was alive, but the dream they had for her life died along with the doctor's words. He was saying that Elizabeth would never go to kindergarten, learn to tie her shoes, roller skate, stay up all night at slumber parties, chatter on the telephone, graduate from high school, attend college, marry, or have babies of her own. They really didn't understand how much they had lost that day. It was pretty vague. Yet Joan and Greg knew that their dream of raising a little girl and experiencing all the typical little girl joys and sorrows was dead. They began to grieve their loss, the loss of a dream and a vision for Elizabeth.

According to modern psychology there are five stages of grief. The first one is denial. Joan and Greg, however, did not experience denial, at least not to the degree that it is typically expressed.

"How could I deny the obvious—that Elizabeth was retarded?" Joan asked. "If she had appeared normal for four to five years and then the reality of mental retardation began to appear, maybe then we would have denied the facts. But for us there was no doubt that we had a problem. There was no denying that Elizabeth was profoundly retarded."

Joan's acceptance of the situation was considered by some to be a form of denial in itself. Some said she must not have realized the severity of the circumstances, to accept them so readily. There was, however, another possibility, another way to explain the attitude that Joan and Greg shared.

Although denial is typically the first stage of grief, even psychologists admit that the intensity and severity of this stage can be controlled to some degree. The key is the presentation of the tragedy—its timing and the presenter himself.

"This anxious denial following the presentation of a diagnosis is more typical of the patient who is informed prematurely or abruptly by someone who does not know the patient well, or does it quickly 'to get it over with' without taking the patient's readiness into consideration."[1]

No one could possibly know Joan better or love her more than God. He was the one who had gently broken the news to her in the stillness of the night. And God's timing is always perfect. Because God revealed what was about to happen to her, her stage of denial was shortened, and perhaps had even been completed by the time the doctor made his announcement on the day of Elizabeth's birth. Perhaps denial had been eliminated altogether.

In a normal grief process, denial is followed by anger. In a situation like this, one can imagine a whole list of people who could have been recipients of Joan's anger. She could have chosen to be angry with her physician. Perhaps he had made an error in treatment that had led to this difficulty. If only he had done his job well.

She could have been mad at the children from whom she had contracted the virus. If only they had stayed home from school. She could have chosen to be angry with the parents of those children. If only they had known their kids were contagious.

She could have been angry with God. If only he had protected her. If only he had not allowed this to happen.

But Joan chose *not* to be angry with her physician, the hospital, the children she had taught, their parents, or with God. Perhaps even more importantly, she chose to be content, not to be jealous of others whose circumstances were more fortunate—whose children were normal.

> Anger is cruel and fury overwhelming,
> but who can stand before jealousy?
> *Proverbs 27:4*

Jealousy is a very powerful and a very negative emotion that wars against our ability to accept all that happens to us as coming from the hands of a good God. Anger and fury in all their magnitude are still outdone by jealousy. Jealousy can ruin a friendship, a family, and the individual who harbors it. It is destructive both to the one who carries it and to the one who is its recipient.

Can you see how Joan might have been tempted to let jealousy breed in her life? Elizabeth would never do the things other little girls do. That certainly was not fair. Joan might have thought about giving up teaching. Perhaps if she simply refused to help any other child develop, Elizabeth's handicap would not appear so great. Why should Joan be interested in teaching concepts and ideas to other parents' perfect, healthy kids when Elizabeth would never be able to learn much of anything? Let their mothers teach them! Why, a child just getting ready to go to school had already learned things that Elizabeth would never learn!

For I have learned to be content
whatever the circumstances.
Philippians 4:11

"God calls me to be content. Not complacent, but content," Joan said. "Comparing Elizabeth with other children is pointless. That's where jealousy begins.

"I suppose that it is like comparing your home with another's or the achievements of your children with the achievements of other people's children.

"The comparisan can lead to arrogance (if you choose to compare to a lesser home or achiever) or to jealousy. After all, you can always find a more palatial dwelling or a more motivated or decorated achiever. I want to be content with what God has allowed to happen. It matters so much more what I do *in* the circumstances than what the circumstances are."

Joan chose contentment versus comparison. She was proactive, not reactive in response to her circumstances. When we are tempted to react in jealousy, we need to remind ourselves to quit comparing, to be accepting, and to learn contentment. Try to begin to see the many reasons you have for contentment. Comparison is a game with no winners.

There were other things that Joan did that helped her choose to accept her circumstances. She chose to exercise her talents rather than her torments. She had been trained as a teacher, and she was a very good one. When I first met her she was teaching kindergarten. Her enthusiasm for children and for learning was exciting and contagious. I remember being in her kindergarten classroom during a lesson on the importance of hand washing to prevent the spread of germs. Joan took a red washable marker and colored a portion of the palm of her hand with it.

"This marker color is just like germs. I need to wash my hands before I eat to wash away the germs," she explained. "Look what happens when I don't."

She shook hands with the children in her class, and one by one their hands turned red as the marker rubbed off on their palms.

"The marker stain is like the germs that are on our hands. Real germs are invisible. You can't see them," Joan explained to her eager students. "And they pass from one person to another very easily. They move just as easily as this marker stain moved from my hand to yours. We need to wash before we eat so that the germs don't get on our food."

The kids understood. They didn't want to be the ones who passed germs to other children.

The lesson was a hit, and as soon as they were allowed, each kindergartner washed off the marker stain with great relish. They didn't want to spread any germs or marker stains!

How ironic, I thought. Little children just like these probably gave cytomegalovirus to Joan. Lovable kids like these gave her the virus that resulted in Elizabeth's retardation. While Joan could have been angry or jealous or discontent, she was not. She just went on doing a great job of teaching this group of young children—teaching them concepts, ideas, and facts that her daughter would never learn, never be able to grasp.

Who would have blamed Joan if she had chosen to lock away her teaching talents and never use them again? Did anyone expect her to invest herself in healthy kids when she had Elizabeth to care for? Who would not have understood if she had chosen to be bitter and to torment herself and others with her pain? Talents or torments—for Joan the choice was clear. Her choice not to be jealous of others and to accept her situation allowed her to exercise her talents in teaching.

Joan chose not to ask "Why?" "Why" questions have no answers. "Why did I get sick when I was pregnant?" "Why was my baby affected by the virus?" "Why is Elizabeth retarded?"

Joan chose to ask "What" questions. "What can I learn from this situation?" "What can I teach others?" "What" questions move us further along in accepting our circumstances.

Joan learned almost immediately the importance of graciously accepting any display of kindness or concern with respect to Elizabeth.

"People responded to Elizabeth in different ways, and they still do," Joan explained. "There are some who greet her cheerfully: 'Oh, hi, Elizabeth. How are you doing?' Then, because of her cerebral palsy, they have to wait for eight to ten seconds for her to respond to them with a smile or a laugh. There are other folks who act as though Elizabeth is invisible. They ask about her in her presence, but never address her personally. And, of course, there are people who avoid any contact or connection with Elizabeth or with me when we are together."

God showed Joan very early how important it was to encourage all those reaching out to her. It is not easy to know what to say to a mother of a retarded child. Joan decided that she would appreciate any attempt at encouragement or consolation even if it was an awkward attempt. She knew that people were trying to minister to her and to

Elizabeth in their own sometimes fumbling ways.

"It is pointless to think less of someone who is uncomfortable," Joan explained. "He or she is responding to the degree of his or her ability to respond. I am just grateful for any acknowledgement of our situation. I've decided to accept any comfort, even if it is misguided. When people say something that could be interpreted as insensitive, I silently say, 'They don't mean this maliciously. They just want to minister to me. OK, they didn't do it just right, but I'm going to take it for what it is—a hand extended in friendship.'"

Joan didn't learn this gracious response on her own. She learned it from God. And she's taught me and others who know her so much about gracious acceptance of the words of others.

She has also taught me that there are no perfect words to speak to someone in crisis or who has had something devastating happen in his or her life. So instead of waiting for perfect words, just say *something* to a hurting person. Do the best you can, and leave the rest to God. This doesn't mean that I charge into a tragedy just to show up. It does mean that as friends experience difficult situations I show them some expression of my caring. The friend who has lost a loved one, or is feeling the pangs of a rebellious child, or is experiencing grief in any form needs to know that I know she hurts and that I care. Joan's example has encouraged me to speak in love.

"When little children see Elizabeth bobbing in her

wheelchair, they wonder what is wrong with her. I smile at them and sometimes even say, 'Elizabeth is retarded. She can see the bright colors in your shirts and she likes them.' These kids are curious, but they are not cruel," Joan explains. "I try to appreciate their attention and encourage it. Elizabeth does."

Joan also learned that even Elizabeth could have a ministry to others. When Elizabeth was seven months old, she and Joan started a physical therapy program called patterning. Joan and Greg's home was located within blocks of the Christian school where Joan had taught. She organized a schedule, asked for volunteers, and the patterning began. Five times a day, for thirty minutes each time, three people provided physical stimulus to Elizabeth. They also laid hands on her and prayed for her. It was a positive experience for everyone involved.

Elizabeth's cheerful countenance and good nature were a blessing to everyone who volunteered. Her appreciative attitude reminded those around her to count their blessings.

"The men and women who came to help me had a real ministry to Elizabeth," Joan said. "I was able to minister to them, and amazingly Elizabeth ministered to them, too. It was an incredible time."

The patterning therapy continued until Elizabeth was two. Then the school relocated, and other factors let Joan know it was time to do something different. What had Joan learned? She had learned that everyone can have a ministry. It is not limited by mental ability.

> I praise you because I am
> fearfully and wonderfully made.
> *Psalm 139:14*

With the birth of Elizabeth, Joan also learned in a first-hand way about the sanctity of human life. And how does Joan feel about pro-life versus pro-choice?

"I was quizzing a candidate for state representative and I asked him his stance on pro-choice or pro-life. 'Oh,' he replied, 'I'm pro-life,' but then he started waffling, 'unless of course the unborn child is retarded. Then the woman should have the right to terminate the pregnancy.'"

He paused, and Joan stepped right in.

"How interesting. I have a severely mentally retarded child. Her name is Elizabeth and I am very grateful that her life was not terminated," Joan replied.

At that point the air was so thick you could cut it with a knife. Joan is very gracious to those who are even slightly uncomfortable with Elizabeth, but she is not tolerant of politicians, policy makers, who are not willing to support the sanctity of *all* human life. Such candidates will never get Joan's support.

When Joan declares that all life is precious, she knows that it is. She comes from a different vantage point than the average citizen or parent. She's had firsthand experience. God has taught her just how precious life is, and now she teaches others.

Joan's grief was proactive. She chose contentment over comparison, talents over torture, and acceptance over jealousy. She asked the question, "What can I learn from this situation that I can in turn teach others?" She saw the importance of appreciating gestures of kindness and teaching others to respond to hurting people in kindness and in love. She learned to acknowledge the potential ministry of people in all stations of life, and to teach others this truth. She also grasped, beyond the average person's ability, the truth of the sanctity of human life.

> A child is a gift whose worth cannot
> be measured except by the heart.
> *Theresa Ann Hunt*

And how did Joan handle the last stages of grief? They are typically viewed as bargaining, depression, and ultimately acceptance.

"I don't believe in the God/rock theory," Joan told me one day. "That's where God sits up in heaven and arbitrarily throws rocks at people. That theory shows God to be capricious and indiscriminate. Like he has no plan for a life."

If you believe in the sovereign power of God, there is no need to bargain. You understand that he has a plan for each life.

And depression? "The day Elizabeth would have gone to school was 'one of those moments' that you have as the mother of a retarded child," Joan explained. "On the first day of kindergarten, Elizabeth, of course, did not attend school. I cried throughout the day as once again the reality of her handicap reared its ugly head. My Elizabeth would never go to 'real school.'"

Instead, Elizabeth attends a class for the profoundly mentally retarded. The ratio of teacher-aide, social worker to student is almost one to one, and Elizabeth gets excellent instruction.

Elizabeth cannot walk. An army crawl takes her from room to room at home. At school and beyond she moves only as someone else pushes her wheelchair. She has a sum total of three words in her vocabulary.

"Elizabeth can't say 'momma' or 'mommy.' Those words take fine motor skills that she has not developed," Joan said. Elizabeth can sign for hungry and thirsty and will occasionally signal when she has to go to the bathroom.

Does all of this depress Joan? She has her moments, but if depression is defined as a condition that impairs normal functioning, then the answer is "no." Elizabeth is mentally retarded and Joan has accepted the fact.

> A mother understands
> what a child does not say.
> *Jewish proverb*

Joan is often asked, "How do you handle a profoundly mentally retarded child?" She tells those who ask, "You help her to be the best she can be, and you try to never get stuck in neutral. I know that God wants me to move forward in life and to grow. I want to grow spiritually and professionally in all areas. He does not want me to blame Elizabeth or use her handicap as an excuse for complacency, anger, or jealousy."

There are no "if only's" for Joan and her family. Would life have been different without Elizabeth? Of course. It might have been much easier. But Joan tells the other side of it. "I might have been arrogant and self-serving without Elizabeth," she says. "Being the parent of a profoundly mentally retarded child is humbling—very humbling," Joan admits. Because she gave birth to Elizabeth, a wonderful young lady who is profoundly mentally retarded, Joan had choices to make, and she chose not to be jealous of those who have it easier because they do not have a disabled child. She chose to be content. Because of her choices and attitude she has made a significant investment in the lives of not only her own children but also those of countless others.

> Love looks through a telescope;
> envy, through a microscope.
> *Author unknown*

8

Choose to Be Flexible

> This world belongs to the man
> who is wise enough to change his mind
> in the presence of facts.
> *Author unknown*

Life doesn't always go as planned. Perhaps it would be more accurate to say that life *very seldom* goes as planned. Darla had a plan as a young girl. She dreamed of growing up and becoming a nurse. At ten years of age she was certain that nursing was her destiny. She admired all the things she knew about nursing. Darla was certain that God had created her to help others through the caring ministry of nursing.

But life does not always go as planned. The oldest of twelve children, Darla grew up in a very stable and loving Christian home. Her father worked hard on their dairy farm and her mother worked hard at preparing Darla and her eleven brothers and sisters for responsible adulthood. The family attended a fundamental church in a town about thirty miles from their farm.

At eighteen Darla was offered a nursing scholarship from a nearby hospital, but the church's stance was that young women did not need to attend college. After all, "the evils of the world are present at college, and it is best to protect our young women from those evils." Furthermore, the church deemed that young women didn't need college skills to be good wives and mothers.

These strong opinions led Darla to decline the nursing scholarship. She wanted to become a nurse, but even more importantly, she wanted to honor God with her choices. She trusted that giving up the scholarship was a more godly choice.

> You need to keep on patiently doing
> God's will if you want him to do for you
> all that he has promised.
> *Hebrews 10:36, TLB*

She took a job at a local bank. The work was adequate, but Darla saw it simply as a holding pattern until she would become a wife and mother. The opportunity to take that step came sooner than she had expected. An elder of the church Darla and her family attended presented her with a proposal from his son. His son was twenty-four years old and had been living in another state for some time. Darla had only visited with him one time since she had become a member of the church.

For those of us who dated and were courted, the prospect of marriage to a virtual stranger seems unthinkable. In the tradition of Darla's faith, however, it was not unusual. After praying long and hard about the proposal, Darla had faith to set a wedding date. She wanted to wait three months so that they could spend a little time together before the wedding, but the church traditionally had shorter engagements so the date was set for six weeks hence.

"A shorter engagement is better," Darla was told. "It lessens the chances of being tempted and falling into sin." So six weeks it was. All that Darla knew about this young man was that he was somewhat attractive, a member of a large family, and the son of the church elder. She was also aware that he had been a little on the wild side in his late teens and early twenties, and, according to his father, "had some trouble holding down a steady job, but seemed ready to settle down now."

Do you have red flags waving all over in your mind? Are there caution signs flashing brightly at the very idea of this young woman getting herself involved like this? She was to become the bride of a virtual stranger.

"I realized on our honeymoon that Ron had severe problems," Darla said. "All I could do was believe that if I loved him enough, and didn't do anything to rock the boat, someday things would be better."

> Blessed are the flexible …
> for they shall not be bent out of shape.
> *Plaque on my wall*

Darla didn't plan to marry an emotionally crippled man. She didn't plan to marry someone with a history of drug abuse and violence, and certainly not someone who chose not to cope with daily life and its pressures. She realized early on in her marriage that she would need to be flexible in order to survive in her situation.

Ron was a violent young man, but initially he did not turn his violence toward her. She learned how to avoid conflict with him.

"He had abused his father on several occasions," Darla said. "I was actually emotionally stronger than Ron's father, and I announced very soon after our marriage that he had better not hit me or I would be gone."

As far as work was concerned, the job Ron got when he returned to his parents' home prior to the wedding lasted for only two weeks after the ceremony. His father had been correct, though he had understated the issue—his son definitely had trouble holding down a job.

> "Be strong and courageous. Do not be terrified; do not be discouraged, for the Lord your God will be with you wherever you go."
>
> *Joshua 1:9b*

Less than two years after the wedding, Darla gave birth to a son. She had been working outside their home to support the family, but with the arrival of Robert, she looked for a job she could do at home. Darla began to sew custom draperies and curtains for a large department store. The job provided some money for the struggling family, but nowhere near enough. Ron worked on and off and ultimately enrolled in a government program to help people develop skills for the workplace. In addition, he began to go to psychological counseling once a week.

"By the time our second child, Marie, was born, Ron had been in a psychiatric unit twice," Darla explained. "We had a very difficult time making ends meet. In order to supplement the money I was making in my sewing business, we tended chickens and gathered eggs for a hatchery."

Although Darla did all she could to keep her family together, it was growing more and more difficult. Was this what God intended for her life?

"I continued to sew drapes, curtains, and bedspreads for the department store," Darla explained, "but we were often overdrawn at the bank, had enormous credit card bills, and still owed for the delivery of both of our children. At one particular time we had no milk, bread, or eggs in the house, only canned green beans."

Darla knew there were government programs available to help people as they worked their way through hard times like these. Finally, in desperation, she applied for Aid to Dependent Children. As she filled out first one form and then another, she answered the questions honestly and in a straightforward manner. Finally, after several visits to the government office, Darla heard the outcome of her many applications.

"Darla," the official began, "you are just the kind of person this program is designed for. You are trying to get back on your feet and I really wish we could help you. I'm sorry, Darla, but as long as you accurately report your income from your sewing business, you will not qualify for financial assistance."

"Are you suggesting that I lie about my sewing money just so I can get help?" she asked with disbelief.

"Well, I'm not exactly saying you should lie," he began.

With that, Darla rose to her feet, took the folder filled with her paperwork, and threw it on his desk. Papers flew everywhere.

"Fine," she said with complete resolve, "you can keep your government money. I'll work for mine!"

This wonderful government program "designed to help people just like Darla" was no help at all. At the moment she realized the truth, Darla had a choice. She could have lied about her income. She could have given up and given in. Things were definitely not going as planned. Darla made the choice not to break but to bend—to be flexible. If government help was not the answer, it did not mean there was *no* answer. If the door to government aid was closed, Darla would look for an open window.

> When God closes a door,
> look for a window.
> *Author unknown*

In December, five and one-half years after Darla and Ron were married, things reached an all-time low. Darla was seven months pregnant with their third child, and Ron was not contributing to the family's finances at all. In fact, he was a financial drain.

Darla's faith was also at an all-time low. How could God desert her? How could he allow her family to come to this destitute state? Christmas would soon be here and she had no money. As Darla walked to the mailbox one day, she cried out to God. "If you are the God I think you are, and if your word is true, then you will provide for us," Darla demanded. "There will be a card with a gift of money in our mailbox."

She opened the mailbox. There was no card and there was no money. As Darla walked back to the house, broken-hearted, she had a thought—a new and fresh thought.

All along she had blamed Ron for their circumstances. After all, it wasn't her fault that he didn't work, had a bad temper, and made everyone's life miserable. This mess they were in was not her fault, it was Ron's. That is what she had always thought—before. But her new thought was something different. Perhaps it didn't matter who was at fault. Perhaps she should stop blaming Ron. Darla decided to take the responsibility for finding some extra work to earn Christmas money.

She called several businesses and asked if they needed any part-time help. She said she would clean, type, wait tables, do anything to earn extra money for Christmas. At first it was difficult to find someone interested in hiring a seven-months-pregnant woman, but one day Darla got a call.

"Darla, have you ever made peanut brittle?" the caller inquired.

"No, I haven't, but I will try," was Darla's response, and her kitchen became a candy factory. She worked all hours of the day and night, and by Christmas she had earned close to $500.

"Even more important than the money I earned," Darla explained, "was the fact that my small seed of faith was watered and started to grow. I once again believed that God had a plan for me and for my children."

> Problems are only opportunities
> in work clothes.
> *Henry Kaiser*

Darla chose to be flexible. She could have been rigid about the type of work she would do, rigid about her work hours, or rigid about her pay scale. Instead, she decided to be flexible and to respond to any opportunity God provided.

Christmas came and went and little Lynn joined her brother Robert and her sister Marie. The increased responsibility of a third child brought things to a head in Darla's home. Ron, who was still going to the job skills program, became angry one day and put his fist through a door at the job skills center. Charges were brought against him and the judge sentenced him to pay for the broken door and spend one weekend in the county jail. During his stay in jail, Darla and her children went to her parents' home. It was then that she gave Ron an ultimatum. If he did not get and keep a job, she and the kids were not coming home.

Ron must have realized, at least initially, that Darla had drawn the final line in the sand. He found a job and managed to keep it for one week, two weeks, three weeks. His resolution continued and he worked for four weeks, five weeks, six weeks, seven weeks. Finally his family returned home. That was in April.

One Friday in July, Ron announced that he was not going to work. He had no reason. He had merely decided to step over Darla's line. He was testing her.

Darla, who was still sewing draperies, had finished a pair and was preparing to go to her client's house to hang them. She loaded the drapes and the kids into the car.

"Darla, go past the shop and tell my boss I won't be in today," Ron ordered. "Oh, and get me a box of Band-Aids."

"Ron," Darla replied as calmly as she could, "you can call your own boss, and go buy your own Band-Aids."

That was all it took to trigger an outrageous explosion from Ron. He chased her out of the house, shrieking obscenities and attempting to seriously hurt her. He took a swing at her and broke the window of their car. The neighbors saw his rage and called the police. Ron was ultimately restrained and Darla pressed charges. On Monday she filed for a legal separation and a restraining order to keep Ron away from her family. In lieu of child support, Ron yielded his half of their house (near foreclosure) to Darla. She was given full custody of their children. Ron became a drifter.

> Under three things the earth trembles,
> under four it cannot bear up:
> [one is] an unloved woman who is married.
> *Proverbs 30:21, 23a*

Life doesn't always go as planned. Darla was alone with her three kids, a house near foreclosure, and more than $30,000 in unsecured debt. Now was not the time to be brittle. Now was the time to be flexible and find a creative solution. She needed a way to crawl out of the hole she found herself in.

Darla personally went to all the people to whom they owed money. She set up a payment schedule and promised a certain amount to each lender—sometimes only five or ten dollars a week. If they would give her a chance, Darla said, she would faithfully strive to fully pay each debt.

Everyone agreed and Darla started the process. She continued to sew draperies and God blessed her business abundantly.

"I remember the month I finished paying my bills and had $30 to spare," Darla said. "I was so excited, I decided to buy a new pair of Sunday shoes."

As she thought about buying new shoes, however, she felt no peace. It was as though God was directing her another way. "I argued with God. It had been seven years since I had bought new Sunday shoes, and that was how I wanted to spend my money," she explained. "But I knew God wanted me to give it away."

So Darla put the $30 in an envelope and anonymously mailed it to a widow in her church who was struggling financially. Later in the week, the most amazing thing happened. Darla received an anonymous envelope with $60 enclosed. Her choice to be flexible and hold her money loosely had been blessed by God. God continued to bless her hard work, giving her a humble spirit and a flexible attitude. God was Darla's provider.

Before long Darla was offered a job as an administrative assistant in a local bank. The job provided a more stable and predictable income for her family than sewing drapes. The only difficulty was that she was still at work when the kids got home from school.

After a few months of this, Darla decided that the job was not as perfect as she had imagined. Just as she was debating about what to do next, she got a call from someone at a bank in a town near her parents' home. The bank had a position available and asked her if she would consider it.

The location change was an answer to her prayers. She could live near her folks and the kids would be able to go to the farm after school and help with chores, and then Darla could pick them up after work.

Darla's ability to be flexible proved an asset once again. The new plan worked well, and the kids flourished living near Darla's kind and loving family.

Darla received a promotion at the bank and then another, but her heart wasn't in banking. In the back of her mind was an idea planted nearly twenty-five years before, the idea that Darla could become a nurse. She began to save $300 a month and put it into a school account. Money was not, however, the only factor to consider. Would she be able to handle the classes, the academic work?

In order to test the water, Darla enrolled in two night

classes at a junior college about fifty miles from her home.

"When I went to register, I drove into the parking lot and thought, 'I can't do this,' and drove out. I drove in and out, in and out, four times before I finally had the courage to park and go in," she explained. "I signed up for psychology and sociology that day, and interviewed for the fall nursing program."

Darla was accepted into the program and initially tried to both work full-time and be a full-time student. She went to classes on Monday, Wednesday, and Friday and worked at the bank on Tuesday, Thursday, and Saturday.

"Usually, when kids go to college they ask for their parents' support. In my case it was just the opposite," Darla explained. "I called my kids together and we sat down at a family meeting. I told them that this college thing had to be a family decision. If I was going to do this, I needed their support."

She got it. Darla's three children were 100 percent behind their mother. Now *they* became the flexible ones.

"Sometimes I had to leave home at 5:00 A.M.," said Darla, "and those three kids would get themselves up and ready for school and the bus."

Ultimately Darla had to give up her banking job in order to dedicate herself to school. Instead she worked part-time at a less demanding job and went to school full-time.

School went well for Darla and she was an honor student. Each year the junior college she attended gave an award called the All-American Student of the Year. It typically went to a student in business or agriculture. It had never gone to a nursing student.

"I was nominated and went through several interviews," Darla recalled. "The last two were with the president of the college." Ultimately Darla was selected for the award.

"I told the president that I could not have gone back to school without the support of my children," said Darla. "I couldn't have done it without their good attitudes and flexibility."

On graduation day Darla was honored, and so were three very special people.

"There are three additional people I want to honor today," the college president began. "Would Robert, Marie, and Lynn please stand? These children helped their mom through college."

Darla's children were honored on that day by the college president. Their mother honors them much more frequently. "God has given me three good kids," Darla said with great emotion. "They are emotionally stable, good kids!"

> If God is for us, who can be against us?
> *Romans 8:31b*

Life doesn't always go as planned. Darla's dream had been to become a nurse. She had the detour of a nightmarish marriage. But even that was not a complete disaster. After all, her three children were a result. And their encouragement and support helped make Darla's dream become a reality.

Darla didn't plan to be rejected for welfare or to be penniless at Christmas, but she did not accept those circumstances as though she were helpless. When a door closed, Darla looked for an open window.

She didn't plan on being $30,000 in debt when she separated from her husband. But she chose to find a plan to chip away at that debt.

So often things don't go as we have planned. This is nothing new. In Exodus we read about the Israelites crossing the sea. Things didn't go as they had planned, either.

"When Pharaoh let the people go, God did not lead them on the road through the Philistine country, though that was shorter" (Exodus 13:17a).

What? God didn't take them on the most direct route? The Israelites wanted to get out of Egypt and into the Promised Land as rapidly as possible—quick and clean. Does that sound familiar? We want the easiest path to happiness in our marriages, the simplest trail to raising great kids, the quickest route to success in our careers. I always try to travel on the most direct path. I want to get to my destination as quickly and simply as possible. On trips, I even highlight the map to ensure the proper route.

But God didn't lead the Israelites on the shortest way. He did not take them on the most direct route. Let's look back in Exodus and read that verse to its completion. "When Pharaoh let the people go, God did not lead them on the road through the Philistine country, though that was shorter. For God said, 'If they face war, they might change their minds and return to Egypt.' So God led the people around by the desert road toward the Red Sea" (Exodus 13:17-18a).

God knew which was the best route for the Israelites. It was not the shortest or the quickest, it was the best. God knows the best path for each of us. His road map is perfect even though it may not be the most direct. When things don't go as we plan, we can choose to be rigid or we can choose to be flexible. We can pout or we can punt. We can whine and fuss and feel put upon, or we can look for an alternate plan. We can try to beat down the closed door or we can look for an open window.

Being brittle and rigid does not change our circumstances. Pouting only makes our faces ugly. Whining and fussing and feeling sorry for ourselves makes us miserable. And beating down a closed door is an awfully difficult (and potentially painful) task. Choosing to be flexible, on the other hand, is the choice for a positive attitude. Punting just might lead to a score. Finding an alternative is helpful. And open windows are much more accessible than closed doors.

Darla did not give up when she realized her marriage was far from perfect and not the marriage she had planned. She chose to find solutions to the best of her ability. Darla did not quit when the welfare agent refused her help or when the mailbox failed to produce a note with money. Instead she looked for other answers to the money pit she was in.

When her husband crossed over her boundaries into predefined unacceptable behavior, she chose to find a way to make it on her own. She chose to be flexible and to follow God's direction when she had extra money. And when the opportunity arose for her to go to nursing school, her children chose to be flexible along with her and to help their mom. Being flexible is a choice, and it is a choice that results in a positive attitude.

> We also rejoice in our sufferings, because we know that suffering produces perseverance; perseverance, character; and character, hope. And hope does not disappoint us.
>
> *Romans 5:3-5a*

9

Choose to Respond

> You have two options…
> You can choose to respond—which is positive.
> Or you can choose to react—which is negative.
> *Zig Ziglar in* Top Performance

R-r-r-r-r-ing! The resounding phone startled Sonnie and Bob awake. Although the clock said a little after 5:00 A.M., it felt like the middle of the night.

R-r-r-r-r-ing! This time the summons caused Bob to jump out of bed and go to the phone.

R-r-r-r … The third ring was cut short as he lifted the handset.

"Hello," Bob said and then paused. "Yes, we have a son named Eric. Yes, he was wearing Reebok shoes. Yes, he was driving a blue Citation. An accident? Where? How is Eric?"

Questions came flooding into Sonnie's mind, too, as she was suddenly wide awake and frightened. The answers to those questions would have to wait for an hour or so. Bob hung up the phone, told Sonnie the few details he had learned, and they dressed as rapidly as they could. As they raced to the hospital, the day was dawning and the nightmare was beginning.

> Therefore, prepare your minds for action; be self-controlled; set your hope fully on the grace to be given you when Jesus Christ is revealed.
>
> *1 Peter 1:13*

Isn't it strange how quickly life can change? One day it can be so calm, peaceful, and predictable, and the next day it can be filled with drama, anxiety, and trauma.

Friday had been one of those calm, peaceful, predictable days. Sonnie had gone to work at her flower shop. Bob was at work on the farm. Their son Eric, home from college for the summer, had put in a full day at his summer job at the high school.

Eric had just finished his freshman year in college at a small school in Tennessee. He had been offered, and had accepted, a full baseball scholarship to Benedictine College in Chicago and was to begin in the fall. It was such an exciting time for him, filled with great expectations.

His summer job had been going well. He worked with nice people and his paycheck was a good addition to his college fund. On Friday, after he deposited his check and did some errands, he went to his mom's shop to visit for a minute.

"I deposited my paycheck after work," Eric reported. "And then I mowed Grandma's lawn. Now I'm going to head home and get cleaned up. Then I'm going to go down to the junior college for my class."

"What time is your class?" his mom asked.

"Not until 7:00 P.M., so I have plenty of time," Eric replied.

"Well, have a good time," Sonnie said. "We'll mow our lawn tomorrow. Bye, honey!"

"Bye, Mom," Eric shouted over his shoulder as he went out the door.

This would be their last conversation for many months.

"Fear not, for I have redeemed you;
I have summoned you by name;
you are mine.
When you pass through the waters,
I will be with you;
and when you pass through the rivers,
they will not sweep over you."
Isaiah 43:1-2a

Sonnie and Bob rushed into the hospital and were greeted by the state police and by medical professionals. The officers tried to explain what had happened at the accident site. It had been a one-car accident with no witnesses, so they pieced the evidence together to the best of their ability.

"It doesn't appear that your son was driving too fast," the officer explained. "Since there were no other cars involved, we feel certain that he merely fell asleep at the wheel and lost control."

"How is he?" Sonnie asked. "Where is he?"

Now it was the physician's turn to reply.

"Eric has suffered a severe closed-wound trauma to his head," the emergency room doctor explained. "We do not expect him to survive more than twenty-four hours. His condition is very tenuous. The next few hours are critical."

Sonnie and Bob were in shock. The news was almost overwhelming. How could something like this have happened to Eric? He was so strong and alert ... a healthy young man anticipating such an exciting future. What were his parents supposed to do now, in light of this terrible, terrible news?

What, indeed, were they to do? They had choices to make. Immediately they began to pray for guidance. They knew that even though their own private world seemed to be spinning out of control, God was still in control.

> Trust in the Lord with all your heart and lean
> not on your own understanding;
> in all your ways acknowledge him,
> and he will make your paths straight.
> *Proverbs 3:5-6*

That night was a long one for Eric's family. His brothers, who lived nearby, joined in the vigil as he struggled through the next twenty-four hours. Their emotions were ragged as they dealt with the fact that Eric might not live.

That kind of harsh reality can evoke many reactions and responses. The most typical reaction is shock and disbelief. *Maybe that wasn't our Eric in the accident. Maybe this is just a bad dream and I'll wake up soon.*

We can react with anger and frustration and list our "if only's." *If only Eric had gone to bed earlier the night before, he wouldn't have been tired enough to fall asleep at the wheel. If only he had taken the truck instead of that little car. If only he hadn't enrolled in summer school.*

We can choose to react with a knee-jerk type of reflex: Something happened that I don't like and BAM!! I'm striking back. Or we can respond. A response is a thinking reply, a reply governed by self-control.

After the initial shock, pain, and disbelief, Sonnie and her family chose to respond rather than to react. During the next twenty-four-hour period, they emotionally released Eric to God.

"We prayed that God's will would be done in Eric's life," Sonnie explained. "Only God knew if it was better for Eric to live or die."

The family chose to respond to the life-and-death situation by asking God to take charge. They chose a thinking reply to the trauma, not a reaction. Their choice to respond, although extremely difficult, was made easier by something that had happened earlier in the year. In February, Eric had given his testimony at their home church and had been baptized.

"I knew I wanted to do it," Eric told his mom after the church service. "What would I say to Jesus if he came back today and looked me in the face and said, 'I died on the cross so you could have eternal life. Why haven't you had the courage to stand up and accept my gift?'"

That evening had been such a glorious blessing for Sonnie and all of Eric's family. He unashamedly declared his love for Jesus. This witness made the events that were to occur months later fall into perspective. True, Eric was hanging between life and death, but his death would merely mean a passing from this life to a better one with Jesus.

With this assurance, Eric's family chose to respond to the tragic events by asking God to have his way.

> Be joyful in hope, patient in affliction,
> faithful in prayer.
> *Romans 12:12*

Eric lived through those twenty-four hours. Miraculously, his vital signs began to stabilize, and before long his respiration and heart rate were almost normal. He was, however, in a coma. He lay in his hospital bed, unable to speak, move, or respond in any way. His body was alive, but his brain, the clearinghouse of the central nervous system, was damaged greatly.

Was this God's will? Sonnie had really believed that initially there were only two options: One—Eric would die and be with Jesus, or two—Eric would regain his health. She hadn't considered the possibility that he would be comatose, at least not for so many days.

The days turned into weeks and the weeks turned into months. Eric did not respond in any manner. Occasionally his body would react with a reflexive action, but months passed with no thinking response.

How does a mother respond in this situation? Daily, Sonnie had to choose response versus reaction, and each day it became more difficult.

"After Eric had been in a coma for six months," Sonnie said, "I realized that my hope was almost spent. It was so difficult not to react in anger or frustration."

And then one day Eric's main physician made a suggestion.

"I think that Eric has fluid around his brain keeping him from responding," said the doctor. "It is possible that if we do surgery and install a shunt into his skull to drain the fluid, we might see improvement. There are, however, two things you must consider. Number one, this surgery may not help Eric at all, and number two, the surgery is extremely dangerous and could end Eric's life."

It was a difficult decision. Eric's parents pondered it with very little peace. Their reaction was to avoid the risk. After all, the two considerations the doctor gave them were both so negative that it was hard to imagine any possible success from the endeavor.

"No, we're not going to give permission for the shunt surgery," they told their older children. "It's just too risky."

"But what have we got to lose?" asked their eldest son. "Eric has not responded to anyone or anything since the accident six months ago. This surgery might give him a chance. How can we choose not to give permission?"

That question started Sonnie thinking. Her oldest son was right. The surgery was not a risk. It was an opportunity. The initial decision not to schedule the shunt surgery had been a reaction, a reflex, and not a thinking-reply response. Now they looked at the options and chose to schedule the surgery.

Eric came through the shunt surgery well. There was, however, no dramatic change. On his rounds each day, Eric's doctor would enter the room and in his booming voice ask, "Well, how's my boy Eric doing today?"

Then Sonnie would answer, "Oh, he's just doing great!"

"Here, Eric," the doctor would bark. "Here's my hand. Squeeze my hand, Eric."

Day after day after day there would be no response and the doctor would continue on to his next patient. But one day things were different.

"Here, Eric. Here's my hand. Squeeze my hand, Eric," the doctor commanded.

And Eric did just that! The look on the doctor's face said it all.

"Well, well, well," he began. "This is quite a Christmas gift for you, Mom and Dad. Eric is beginning to respond."

After months in an impenetrable coma, Eric responded with

a squeeze of his doctor's hand. The risky surgery had indeed made a difference. Eric's progress was painfully slow. Nothing changed overnight or dramatically. In tiny, tiny increments he continued to improve. At the one-year anniversary of his near-fatal accident, he still was unable to speak, although he was regaining some ability to move. Time marched on and Eric worked very hard to move forward in his therapy.

> A man's wisdom gives him patience.
> *Proverbs 19:11a*

At times Sonnie had a terrific struggle with patience. Hadn't she been patient enough? It had been six months, eight months, twelve months, and now sixteen months, and still Eric had not spoken one word. It was difficult to keep choosing to respond to Eric and to his situation.

On Thanksgiving weekend, nearly eighteen months after the accident, Eric was allowed to come home for an overnight stay. His motor skills had improved to the point that he could sit up in his wheelchair. He was aware of his surroundings, recognized his family, and obviously enjoyed being with them. He was, however, on a feeding tube and still could not speak a word.

Sonnie was nervous, but the overnight visit went well. The next afternoon, Eric's father packed up his things and took him back to the hospital. It was a long drive, so he planned to spend the night and drive back home the next day. Several hours after he and Eric had left, Sonnie received a phone call from them. The trip had been uneventful. They had arrived back at the hospital and Eric was settling in.

"Oh, and I have a little surprise for you," said Eric's father, Bob. "Eric, Mom is on the phone. Here, listen to Mom say hi."

"Hi, Eric!" Sonnie said cheerfully. "It's Mom. It was great to have you home for Thanksgiving. I love you."

"M – m – a —— m," Eric said into the receiver.

Eric said? Yes, he was speaking. It was not easy to understand, but he was saying something. He was saying "Mom."

Eric was responding to his therapy. Parts of his brain were slowly healing.

Eric's recovery continued to provide both him and his mother with opportunities to respond. Eric's response was what every doctor, nurse, and therapist was striving for. Sonnie's responses were choices she had to make daily. Each day she had the option to react or to respond. Her goal was to respond, to give a thinking reply to Eric and to those around him.

Early in the rehabilitation process one of Eric's physicians had told Sonnie that the old Eric was gone. Sonnie's initial reaction to that statement was to refuse to believe it.

"Eric will get better," she thought. "My old Eric will be back."

Sonnie didn't want to even entertain the thought that the Eric she had known and loved for nineteen years was gone forever. That thought was much too painful.

Slowly, however, she realized that perhaps the physician had been correct. Sonnie's denial did nothing to change the situation. Perhaps it was even doing harm.

"One day I realized that my old Eric was truly gone, and that the doctor was right when he said he'd never return," Sonnie admitted. "It was then I chose to let go of the old Eric, so that there was room for the new one. I chose to get to know and love my new son."

Sonnie went from reaction to response. She allowed the new Eric to become her son. "I like the new Eric," Sonnie told me. "He has got to be one of the most pleasant and thankful people I have ever known. He's so grateful, even for little things like singing in church or eating dinner. He thanks his dad and me all the time."

I've gotten to know the new Eric, and I like him, too. Anyone would! He is a hard worker, with God's direction, determination, and perseverance. After eleven years he has regained more and more physical ability. It is still extremely difficult for Eric to communicate verbally, although it is not impossible for him to speak and be understood.

Eric can now walk without a walker or crutches, although his right side is partially paralyzed. He has learned to eat with his left hand, and his smile, though perhaps a little crooked, is very engaging. His mother is right, Eric is pleasant and thankful.

One evening, Sonnie, Eric, and I were enjoying a pizza together when we heard his dad's truck pull up the lane. "I'll bet that's Dad," Sonnie said to Eric. "Maybe he is taking a break from picking corn."

"Da – aaad," Eric repeated with great joy and excitement. "Daaad."

Eric rose slightly from his seat to see if it was his father coming in. Eric's response was pure, unashamed joy. He could hardly wait to see his dad.

Sonnie's response was delight. She loved her new Eric and enjoyed sharing in his excitement that Dad was home.

> O Lord, you have searched me and you know me. You know when I sit and when I rise; you perceive my thoughts from afar.
>
> *Psalm 139:1-2*

We all have so many opportunities each day to choose either to react or to respond. Usually events aren't as monumental or as long-playing as Sonnie's and Eric's. We react or respond to our families, our coworkers, the people we meet in the grocery store. Responding means controlling the tongue.

> He who guards his lips guards his life.
>
> *Proverbs 13:3a*

Years ago I headed up a team of workers putting together a convention. There were many details that were important to the success of the convention. In order to assure that we would attend to those details efficiently and effectively, I developed an easy plan. At our team meetings I would ask for volunteers to accept the various responsibilities. As people volunteered, I would note their names on my list at the same time I saw them adding the task to their lists. That, I thought, would assure that every base was covered and no detail would be forgotten.

The week of the convention finally arrived and things were going smoothly. One particular detail that a team member had written on her list was the purchase of poster board for one of our speakers. Judy had volunteered for that task and about forty-five minutes before this particular speaker was to appear, I approached Judy to ask where she had put the poster board.

"You never told me to buy poster board," she said defensively.

Now, I knew for a fact that I had indeed asked her to buy poster board. I had made a note of it on my list when I saw her put it on her list. I had to fight the overwhelming urge to react. I could have said, "I *know* you volunteered to get poster board. There is no doubt in my mind. You just *forgot*, didn't you?"

I could have said that. It would not have been very kind or considerate. It would not have been a thinking reply. And it would not have gotten me poster board. Instead, through the grace of God, I said to myself, "Kendra, what is your goal?" That question, by the way, is an excellent way to increase your chances of responding rather than reacting.

What was my goal? That's right! It was to get poster board. So, instead of ranting and raving and proving that I was right and she was wrong, I took a deep breath and said, "Whew! We need poster board. Do you think you can find any?"

"Well," she said, "I could probably take the rental car and run down the block to the discount store."

"Great idea," I replied and off she went.

The poster board arrived in plenty of time. The speaker was a happy camper and so was my coworker. Thank goodness I remembered to ask myself, "What is my goal?" That was a good choice, and it sent me in the direction of a positive attitude.

Unfortunately I don't always make that good choice. Sometimes I choose to react. On one particular evening in early February, I witnessed a very distressing basketball game. Our eldest son, who was sixteen at the time, played on a team that was young and inexperienced. That night they were matched with a much more physical and accomplished team. The result was a frustrating, one-sided game. Way beyond the impact of the score, however, was the fact that our young players were bombarded with nasty comments and unkind remarks throughout the game. It was a very negative experience.

When the game finally ended, our son grabbed his coat, trousers, and gym bag and told his coach he was riding home with us. He was exhausted from spending the evening in this demoralizing situation. As our family walked outside, the boys and my husband, John, were a few feet ahead of me. The cold air hit my face, and I suddenly realized that Matthew had not put his coat on yet.

"Matthew, put your coat on," I told him.

This eldest child who usually responded in an immediate manner did nothing. His sweaty, slumping shoulders remained uncovered.

"Matthew, it's cold outside. Please put your coat on," I repeated.

When there was still no response, I prepared to give the order a final time with more conviction. As I began to speak, my second son, Aaron, slipped back a few steps to walk with me.

He reached over, touched my arm, and said, "Mom, you've got to know when to hold 'em and know when to fold 'em."

Wow! Wisdom out of the mouths of babes (teens actually). Aaron was 100 percent correct. I was reacting. I wasn't giving a thinking response. If I had been thinking, I would have realized that at that moment, Matthew did not need my advice about dressing for conditions. Instead he needed the assurance of my unconditional love.

What was my goal? Aaron reminded me to ask that question. Sometimes it takes a little reminder from a loved one to help us choose to respond rather than to react.

> Not only to say the right thing in the right place, but far more difficult, to leave unsaid the wrong thing at the tempting moment.
>
> *Author unknown*

Sonnie chose to respond to the initial shock of Eric's accident rather than to react in anger. Sonnie and her family found peace through their faith in God. Sonnie needed the reminder of her older children to help her respond to the decision about Eric's shunt surgery. Her reaction was "no." Her response—

her thinking reply—was "yes." And finally Sonnie chose to respond to the new Eric by letting go of the old Eric and making room for her "new" son.

Sonnie responded. She chose faith-filled, thinking replies. She could have chosen to react to Eric's accident and to his long and continual recovery period. Even today she could choose to react to his limited abilities, or she could choose to respond. Sonnie chose to respond and continues to make the choice to respond to circumstances beyond her control with love, joy, and enthusiasm. And Eric responds to her.

"Every day I have a choice to spend the day indulging in self-pity or allowing the Lord to have victory as he refines me for his kingdom," Sonnie explained. "And I am here to tell you that God is able. When our hearts are broken by tragedy, Jesus holds every piece of our broken heart and if we allow him, he will put each piece back together with his everlasting glue."

10

Choose to Have a Vision

> The most pathetic person in the world
> is someone who has sight but no vision.
> *Helen Keller*

In its simplest terms, having a vision is seeing or setting a mark in the distance and moving toward it. Jean Driscoll has had a vision of one kind or another—a mark in the distance—that she has pursued since she was two years old. Born with spina bifida, Jean's prognosis was bleak. The doctors told her parents that she would never walk. Furthermore, they suspected that she would have learning difficulties and that she would be dependent on her parents all of her life. The physicians couldn't have been more wrong. If you want Jean Driscoll to do something, just tell her she can't and she will.

At the age of two, this child who was told she would never walk developed her own means of locomotion. Her very efficient hands-and-feet crawl convinced her mother, a trained nurse, that Jean might be able to walk with below-the-knee braces. So she purchased braces and her first vision—the first mark in the distance—was reached. Jean walked! She had been determined, and she had accomplished her goal.

A few years later Jean was enrolled in school—the same one her sister had attended earlier. To her parents' delight she had *no difficulty* with academic work. What was it that the doctor had said about mental deficiency? Jean had no mental deficiency.

> A goal properly set is halfway reached.
>
> *Author unknown*

In many ways a vision and a goal are similar. A vision sharpens our focus. It helps us evaluate our choices. The teenager who envisions attending college and ultimately having a career will be less likely to risk the chance of destroying that vision by engaging in self-destructive behavior such as drugs, alcohol, and illicit sex. The young couple with a vision of parenting a healthy child will refuse to take drugs because they might harm their unborn or yet-to-be-conceived child. The woman who has a vision, who has formulated a goal, has, in essence, drawn a target for her life and actions. Hitting the bull's-eye on the target obviously represents the perfect accomplishment of her goal, but even when a bull's eye is missed, there is something to be said for getting close.

> Dissatisfaction and discouragement are not caused by the absence of things but by the absence of vision.
>
> *Author unknown*

Jean's accomplishment of walking was the first of many goals she was able to achieve. Her "prove you wrong" attitude was something she adopted as a means of survival. Early in life she had learned valuable lessons of perseverance and determination.

"I really believe that the trials and struggles I had built strength and character and made me a survivor," Jean said. "Actually they have made me an overcomer."

One day, when Jean was in the fourth grade, her best friend, Marcia, rode to Jean's home on a two-wheel bike she had just mastered.

"I couldn't believe Marcia could ride a two-wheeler," Jean exclaimed. "She was two years younger than me and I still had training wheels."

Jean was sure that she could ride a two-wheel bike, too. And so on Saturday, she spent the day—all eight hours of it—at Marcia's house, developing her balance and practicing until she could successfully ride to her own house.

"Mom, Mom, I can ride a two-wheeler," Jean shouted as she entered the house.

"No, you can't," her mom replied.

"Yes, I can," Jean said, undaunted. "Come to the door and watch me."

Jean hurried outside to the waiting bicycle. "Don't get on that thing," Jean's mother warned. "You're going to break your neck."

Jean ignored her mother's warning and got on the bike. "Just watch me," she reassured. "Watch me." She was so excited as she rode around and around the family driveway.

As her mother watched in amazement, she simply said, "Well, I guess when your dad gets home from work, he can take the training wheels off your bike."

Jean had a vision—a vision of herself on a bicycle without training wheels—and she did what it took to capture that vision and attain that goal. Biking skills served Jean well for the next several years. She had freedom and speed that she had only imagined she might one day have. And then one day while riding home on a new ten-speed bike she had won in a muscular dystrophy read-a-thon, Jean took a corner too sharply and crashed into the pavement. The accident dislocated her hip, but it quickly popped back in and Jean got on the bike and rode home.

"I really didn't think it was too bad," Jean recalled. "It burned a little, but I put it out of my mind until later when I tried to go up the stairs to answer a phone call." Her hip immediately dislocated once again, and this time the pain was more intense. The biking accident was much more serious than Jean had imagined.

"I fell on Wednesday and I went to school the next two

days on crutches," Jean said. "On Saturday we went to see the doctor. I can still remember him saying, 'This is quite a debacle, isn't it, Jean?' It was years later before I had any idea what a debacle was."

It certainly was a debacle, for Jean went to the hospital the very next day and spent the next year in and out of it. She had several surgeries and spent close to a year in a body cast. The doctors did everything they could to repair and restore her hip joint, but the socket was too shallow, and her lower body musculature too undeveloped because of the spina bifida.

After the doctors finally claimed that they had done all they could, Jean was sent home to recuperate. The first week she was home, she sat up in bed and dislocated her hip again. Can a fifteen-year-old establish or maintain a vision in the light of all these setbacks? The surgeries had been painful and the recovery in the body cast was tedious. Jean had lost more than a year and a half of high school.

She was determined to walk again. She thought, *I can do this. I can go through all of this because I'm going to be able to walk again. That is the most important thing to me. Walking is everything.*

As Jean vowed to walk again, she concentrated on that vision, analyzing how she could reach her goal. She even tried to learn to walk without crutches. But that target was one she would never hit.

"I concentrated hard but I could only go a couple of steps. When I walked prior to dislocating my hip, my feet were turned outward," Jean explained, "and I dragged them because I didn't have the muscles to lift them. I didn't understand the whole balance thing. I didn't understand the whole spina bifida thing. I just knew I walked funny. I never understood my disability—why things didn't work."

The next few years were difficult for Jean. She ultimately had no choice but to use a wheelchair and crutches. And even though academics had always come easily to her, she began to struggle in school. Her failure in school and her lack of options in getting around on her own were devastating, and she felt defeated and discouraged.

"I was very angry at God," Jean said. "'Why don't you pick on somebody else?' I asked him."

Jean's anger was, at this point, her only emotion toward God. She had never really met him and so did not know him or love him. But God knew her and he loved her greatly. He loved her so much that he allowed her not to walk. He had a plan for her that included a wheelchair.

> Forgetting those things which are behind,
> and reaching forth unto those things
> which are before.
> *Philippians 3:13, KJV*

During this time, Jean learned about wheelchair athletics.

"I had a bad image of wheelchair sports—one that I had conjured up all on my own. When I finally went to check it out, I was amazed. This was no tea party. There were chairs banging into each other and athletes flying all over," Jean explained enthusiastically. "And no one was gasping or running over to help. These folks were true competitors."

And it was the competitive aspect of the wheelchair sports that appealed to Jean's "prove you wrong" attitude. After her first introduction to the sport, she was hooked.

Jean's target—her vision—became centered on sports and on top performance. In fact, her focus became so narrow that she failed to keep up with her schoolwork at the University of Wisconsin-Milwaukee and she flunked out of school.

To add to her feelings of failure, Jean began to develop serious pressure sores because of the extensive amount of time spent in her chair. The next six months were spent, once again, in and out of the hospital. When she was finally released, Jean went to work for one of the nurses who had become her friend during the numerous days, weeks, and months she had spent in the hospital. The nurse had a young family and recruited Jean as a mother's helper.

Jean moved in with the family and took over many of the household duties. This was a churchgoing family. Actually, they were more than just churchgoers, they were Christians, and Jean started attending church with them. As a result of this, she accepted Christ as her Savior.

"I felt a big relief," Jean remembers. "I now knew I was going to heaven, but it didn't really affect my daily life. I still didn't feel forgiven. I still didn't feel very loved. I still didn't understand the abounding, amazing grace of God."

This was in November of 1986. Still active in athletics, Jean had competed in her first race earlier in 1986 in a very outdated racing chair. In spite of the antiquated equipment and Jean's lack of formal training, she performed well. With a little training and a decent chair, Jean realized, she had the potential to be a winning wheelchair racer. This became the next vision Jean would pursue.

Three months later, Jean received her own racing chair—a vast improvement over the borrowed model she had been using. A wealthy businessman had learned of her talent and need, and had purchased the chair for her. Later, this same man provided her with an airplane ticket to Phoenix to participate in her first national-level wheelchair competition.

"Even with all the amazingly positive events occurring, I didn't see God's hand. When I look back," Jean admits, "I don't have a single doubt that he was leading the way."

> It is a mistake to look too far ahead.
> Only one link of the chain of destiny
> can be handled at a time.
> *Winston Churchill*

Isn't it ironic that the thing Jean rejected with the most vehemence, a wheelchair, would become so significant in fulfilling God's purpose in her life? Paradoxes. The Bible is filled with them. We give to receive (see Luke 6:38). We die to live (see Romans 6:8). We pray for those who persecute us (see Matthew 5:44). And in Jean's case she ceased to walk so that she could run—in a wheelchair.

> Man's limitations are God's opportunities.
> *Jean Driscoll*

Jean isn't sure when she first realized the truth in her statement above. She's always been an achiever, someone who persevered, someone with a vision and a goal. But those goals had not always been reached. Her fortitude had not always been enough and had not always been healthy.

Jean's limitations in walking led her to a tremendous opportunity. In the fall of 1986, Jean found herself being earnestly recruited by the University of Illinois (U. of I.) wheelchair basketball coach. There were no scholarships to offer her, just the opportunity to attend a quality university and play on an all-women's basketball team (a unique opportunity at the time). Jean didn't know if she could handle the academics at the U. of I., so she enrolled for a semester at a smaller university in Milwaukee and then accepted the basketball invitation. Jean felt a strange tug on her heart to pursue a collegiate experience at U. of I.

Now Jean had a new vision, a new focus, and it was twofold:

1. Do *not* flunk out of college, and
2. Do not get another pressure sore.

She applied her Driscoll determination to these two goals and was once again successful.

Although she was recruited for basketball, she had achieved success in wheelchair racing. Jean became a two-sport athlete. Her University of Illinois wheelchair basketball team won the national championship in 1990 and 1991, and her racing experience was blossoming in those years, too.

Before long her racing coach convinced her to train for and run a marathon. The idea did not initially appeal to Jean, but out of respect for her coach, she agreed to do one marathon.

> I keep under my body;
> and bring it into subjection.
> *1 Corinthians 9:27, KJV*

A marathon, that's 42 kilometers … 26.2 miles! Jean had said she would run it, and the training began. It was grueling, but her coach felt certain that Jean's upper body strength, developed in part by eight years on crutches, would be a bonus to her.

Jean raced in the Chicago Marathon and earned second place. Relieved that she had done what she had promised, she was unprepared for what her coach told her. Her performance had been so good that she had qualified to run the Boston Marathon.

"What?" Jean asked in disbelief. "I have no intention of running that marathon. I told you I'd do *one* marathon and I've done it."

But Jean's coach prevailed once again and Jean's vision became focused on the running of the Boston Marathon.

> In a race, everyone runs but only one person gets first prize. To win the contest you must deny yourselves many things that would keep you from doing your best.
>
> *1 Corinthians 9:24a, 25, TLB*

In April of 1990, Jean Driscoll ran the Boston Marathon, earned first place in the Women's Wheelchair division, and set a course and world record. This amazing accomplishment exceeded even what Jean, the hard-driving athlete, had set as her target goal. She had more than hit her bull's-eye.

She went on to win a second Boston Marathon and set more records in 1991. That same year she was selected as the Women's Sports Foundation Sportswoman of the Year. This award was significant in many ways. It was very prestigious and desirable. Among the finalists the year Jean won the honor was Kristi Yamaguchi, champion figure skater. But even more important was how God used the award to bring Jean's heart completely to him.

Not long after the presentation of the award, the University of Illinois and the communities of Champaign and

Urbana wanted to honor Jean. The athletic department assigned a new assistant to work with her to ultimately organize a Jean Driscoll Day. The new assistant was a Christian. As the two women worked together on the event, they became friends, and before long Jean was eager to know more about the obvious relationship her friend had with Christ.

Jean attended church for the first time in many years and found a family to nurture her and help her grow. At this point, she recommitted her life to Jesus Christ.

With a new passion for Jesus and an athletic career on the rise, you might think that Jean would finally have a vision or target drawn by Christ.

"I guess I had two separate visions driving my life," Jean explained. "I had my vision and goals for racing, and my vision for my walk with Christ. They functioned independently of one another."

They *were* independent, but only for awhile. Jean's athletic success was on the move. She won the Boston Marathon again in 1992 and 1993. She also earned the Silver Medal in the eight-hundred-meter wheelchair exhibition event at the Olympic Games in Barcelona, Spain, setting the American record.

And then in 1994, Jean drove her van to Boston more prepared than ever to win, and hopeful of setting another course and world record in the marathon.

"I went into Boston stronger than I'd ever been in my life. I was sure that I'd break the world record," Jean told me. "And then two days before the marathon I came down with food poisoning."

On Friday before Marathon Monday, Jean, her coaches, and their families had gone out to eat and had all experienced food poisoning. "Sunday I was lying on my bed, completely worried about what was going to happen the next day. Was I going to be healthy enough to do this race?" Jean recalled.

Reading her Bible, she came to Proverbs 16:3, "Commit to the Lord whatever you do, and your plans will succeed."

"So right then and there I committed the race to him," Jean said.

God's Word had spoken to Jean. Finally her vision for racing and her vision for her spiritual life were merging. She wanted his vision, his goals, and his target for her life.

"I committed that race, the next race, the Olympics, and everything to him," Jean laughed. "It was pretty funny."

The next day was Marathon Monday. Jean got up and was feeling better. She realized that she was feeling good enough to race. It didn't take long once the gun went off and the race began, however, for Jean to realize that she was much weaker than during the workouts she'd put in the week before. Being sick had definitely taken something out of her. She was nervous while trying to get through the warm-up period.

"I got about 10K into the marathon. I was at 6.2 miles and there were 20 more miles in the race. I was feeling so sick I wanted to pull out. I even tried to figure out where I was going to do it. Then all of a sudden I remembered, 'You can't pull out. You committed this race to God.'"

She couldn't pull out, so she kept going. Jean threw up three times during that race and ended up winning by only 23 seconds. That was the closest margin of victory she had ever experienced at the Boston Marathon. But she also set a new world record of 1.34.22.

> Adversity causes some men to break;
> others to break records.
> *Author unknown*

"That marathon was three years ago," Jean said. "Now I commit every workout, every race, every interview, every speaking engagement, every thing to God. That way I know that I will give my best and his Holy Spirit will help me with words and wisdom and humility."

> Let us lay aside every weight, and the sin
> which doth so easily beset us, and let us run
> with patience the race that is set before us.
> *Hebrews 12:1b, KJV*

Jean has now won seven Boston Marathons. Most of us will never win one. Jogging in the one-mile fun run/walk at the Sweetcorn Festival is the height of my athletic achievement at this stage of my life. I will never win a medal in the Olympic Games (although I know I'll cry with the winners as our national anthem is played). I will set no course or world records, but I still share a vision, a dream, a goal with Jean Driscoll, world-class wheelchair athlete. You and I can share the vision and goal of committing all we do to God. Jean did not let an "if only" control her life. No "if only" blocked her from setting goals or committing her vision to God. I can commit my writing, my speaking, my marriage, my parenting, and all aspects of my life to God also. I can ask him for his vision for my life. This vision, this very large lifetime vision, will keep me headed in the right direction. And the smaller, less formidable, short-term visions, like accomplishing the daily tasks God has given me to do, will help me make the right choices.

> Where there is no vision
> the people perish.
> *Proverbs 29:18a, KJV*

Jean learned that with God's vision, people do not perish, they thrive. They are overcomers. And that is a lesson for us all. Choose to have a vision.

> Vision is the world's most desperate need.
> There are no hopeless situations, only people
> who think hopelessly.
> *Author unknown*

11

Other Good Choices

When you look for the good in others
you discover the best in yourself.
Martin Walsh

I taught school for several years before my husband and I started our family. One year I had a group of fourth-graders who did not get along well. They argued and fussed with one another almost all the time. They were respectful to me and were good listeners, but they bickered endlessly with each other.

On one especially rough day, their arguing had pushed me to the edge. I'd had it with their bad attitudes. About three minutes before recess, I asked the class to take out paper and pencils.

"Please write your name at the top of your paper," I began. "On the next line I want you to write the name of the one person you would least like to sit by. Keep your papers covered."

"Do we only write one name?" many asked.

"Can I make a list?" asked one particularly disagreeable young man.

"Just one name," I replied and paused until the task was completed by everyone in class. "Now, number 1, 2, 3 on your paper and write three good things about the person you named. Write three things you could honestly praise about that person."

From the response of the students you would have thought I had just asked them to climb Mount Everest—barefooted!

"I can't!"

"That's impossible!"

Knowing something about motivation and about fourth-graders, I replied, "And as soon as you are done, you may go outside for recess."

Needless to say, they all completed the assignment. Now, I would like to tell you that our little exercise revolutionized the classroom; that things were never the same again; that the students had respect and appreciation for one another for the rest of the year. I would like to tell you this, but I can't because I would be lying. They did, however, treat one another more kindly for a while. It did make a positive (if not eternal) difference in their attitudes and their interactions. Under my direction, those students chose to praise someone else and the arguing subsided. Choosing to praise another person is a good choice for a positive attitude.

CHOOSE TO PRAISE SOMEONE

Giving honest, genuine praise to others has amazing consequences. We often sport a negative attitude when we are focused on ourselves.

"I want it *my* way."

"That's not what *I* want."

"Shouldn't that be for *me*?"

Focusing on someone else, praising someone else, helps to foster a positive attitude. And it is a choice. We make the choice whether or not to praise the people in our lives.

> I will proclaim the name of the Lord.
> Oh, praise the greatness of our God!
> *Deuteronomy 32:3*

Even more importantly, we can choose to praise God. "God inhabits the praises of his people" (Psalm 22:3, KJV). He lives there in our praises! If you ever feel removed from God, away from his presence, his Word says that if we praise him, he is there.

The vacation Bible school kids sing a little song that talks about praising God and how much better that makes them feel. Why? Because when we praise God, we take our focus off *our* selves, *our* lives, *our* hurts, and *our* desires, and shift the focus to God. That little VBS song is packed with truth.

One day, years ago when our two oldest boys were quite

young, we were having family devotions. Now before you get a serene picture of two freshly scrubbed boys sitting reverently and angelically and hanging on every word spoken by their parents, let me tell you that I have been known to refer to our family devotions as "Devotion Commotion." My recollection is that no one was reverent, angelic, or "hanging" that day. Nevertheless, the Word of God was being spoken, and God tells us that "His Word will not return void" (Isaiah 55:11, KJV). Anyway, during family devotions we read the story about Peter walking on the water (see Matthew 14:25-31).

When we finished, one of the boys paused briefly and then declared, "I know why Peter sank."

I must admit that although I, like every young mother, was certain that I was raising above-average children, I couldn't believe that one of the boys thought he knew the answer to the great spiritual and metaphysical question, Why did Peter sink? Nevertheless I played along.

"OK," I said. "Why do you think Peter sank?"

"That's easy," he replied. "He quit lookin' at Jesus."

That was it, nothing more and nothing less. As I pondered this theological conclusion, I read back through the Scripture. "But when he [Peter] saw the wind, he was afraid and, beginning to sink, he cried out, 'Lord, save me!'" (Matthew 14:30).

Translation? Peter quit "lookin' at Jesus" and he sank. His focus shifted from Jesus back to himself, then to the wind and glub, glub, glub, down he went.

How true is that for me? When am I on top of things? When I'm lookin' at Jesus! When I am focusing on him and praising him rather than looking at myself and my circumstances, I am on top of things.

A woman I have known for years faces a very difficult situation with her aging mother. As an only child, all of the responsibility for her mother's care has been hers alone. I know that at times it has been overwhelming. Yet, through the power of praise, my friend has persevered. She listens to hymns of praise and Scripture songs and chooses to focus on Christ. She's "lookin' at Jesus" so that she will not sink. Her attitude is positive as she praises the Lord in her circumstances. Praise is a good choice for a positive attitude.

CHOOSE TO GIVE

> When you help someone up a mountain,
> you'll find yourself close to the summit too.
> *Author unknown*

Do you want a prescription for a negative attitude? I once heard someone say, "Get all you can and can all you get." Now that philosophy is guaranteed to create a negative attitude.

So often we think of giving in terms of our finances. Many times giving money is the easy way to fill a square.

There are many other things we can give. We can give our time, talents, and enthusiasm. Just recently several of our friends gathered together to help our family with a project. As I expressed my gratitude to each one of them, I was overwhelmed by the realization that they gave us the gift of their time. That is a precious commodity, and unlike some resources, it is limited—there are only twenty-four hours in each day.

> Whatever you do, work at it with all your heart,
> as working for the Lord, not for men.
> *Colossians 3:23*

When was the last time you gave the gift of enthusiasm to someone? What about giving away encouragement? God is very clear that he wants us to encourage one another.

> Therefore encourage one another and build
> each other up, just as in fact you are doing.
> *1 Thessalonians 5:11*

The last part of that verse is interesting. "Just as in fact you are doing." Here God is doing exactly what he wants *us* to do. He is encouraging us to be encouragers.

"Great work!" says God. "You're doing a super job encouraging each other. Keep building each other up just as in fact you are doing."

We can be like our heavenly Father and choose to give away encouragement.

> The prayer of a righteous man
> is powerful and effective.
> *James 5:16b*

What about prayer? Do you give prayer away? Several years ago a high school Sunday school class was asked how many of them ***knew*** someone prayed for them each day. A very small percentage had that assurance. Pray for your kids and let them know you're doing it.

One Sunday I arrived at church and was greeted by a person with an unusual question. "What was happening at your house at about 3:20 last night?" the older woman asked me as I walked into church.

"Do you mean 3:20 A.M.?" I asked. "Boy, nothing as far as I know."

"Well," she continued, "God woke me up and led me to pray for you."

"Thanks!" I said enthusiastically.

Who knows what was going on at 3:20 in the early morning. I am not even sure I want to know. All I know is that any harm that might have come to me or to my family was averted. Praise God! I am so thankful that my older friend chose to be a giver and to pray.

> Faith comes from hearing the message, and the message is heard through the word of Christ.
> *Romans 10:17*

Not only can you give away prayer, you can give away your faith too. Years ago I heard a wonderful children's sermon. All the children were gathered at the front of the church when the pastor carried in a great big birdcage covered with a cloth.

"Under this cloth there is a very nice birdcage," he said. "Do all of you know what kind of animal lives in a birdcage?"

"A bird," they said, almost in unison.

"That's right!" he replied, "and I have a big gray bird in my birdcage."

Then he removed the cloth to reveal a big gray *cat* comfortably nestled in the bottom of the birdcage.

"That's not a bird," giggled the young children. "That's a cat."

"It must be a bird," the pastor countered. "It's in a birdcage, isn't it?"

"It's a cat," the children argued. "It doesn't matter if it's in a birdcage or not. It's a cat."

"Oh," the speaker said, obviously enlightened by the wisdom of the preschoolers. "Do you mean that sitting in a birdcage does not necessarily make you a bird?"

"Right!" they answered cheerfully, pleased to have won the battle.

"I guess you're right," he admitted. "And sitting in a church does not necessarily make you a Christian. You must know Jesus as your Savior."

That children's sermon made sense. The gospel message had been presented. Faith had been shared.

Many years later, one of the young people who had heard that children's sermon was asked to present a lesson at his high school Fellowship of Christian Athletes huddle. His lesson was remarkably similar to the one he had experienced as a young child.

The young man had a candle he wanted to light, so he took out a box labeled "Kitchen Matches." When he opened the box he discovered it was filled with thumbtacks. Try as he might, he couldn't light the candle with the tacks.

"Being in a matchbox doesn't make you a match," he concluded. "Living in a garage doesn't make you a car. And sitting in church doesn't make you a Christian. You must know Jesus as your Savior."

That young man took the opportunity that evening to give away his faith, and his timing had eternal consequences. Weeks later a young girl who had attended that meeting was in a fatal car accident. The girl's mother told me that her daughter had not been the same after the FCA meeting. She came home, retold the lesson, and then discussed it at length with her parents, who were both Christians.

"I feel certain that Andrea accepted Christ as a result of that young man's lesson," her mother said. "Now I can look forward to seeing her in eternity."

We can choose to give away our faith.

> The love in your heart
> wasn't put there to stay.
> Love isn't love till you give it away.
> *Author unknown*

We can also choose to give away love, joy, wisdom, and memories. God has given us so much to share. And he wants us to share his gifts to us generously with others.

> Give, and it will be given to you.
> A good measure, pressed down, shaken
> together and running over, will be poured
> into your lap. For with the measure you use,
> it will be measured to you.
> *Luke 6:38*

This verse came alive to me one day as I imagined each end of the giving continuum in a visual way. On one end (the stingy end) I imagined someone giving away love with a McDonald's stirring spoon—a spoon whose bowl was about the size of the fingernail on my smallest finger. God takes that little, bitty spoon, packs love into it, and presses it down. Then he shakes it together so a little more love will fit. And finally he adds more love until it is running over. It's not a big spoon, mind you, but he has packed it fuller than we ever imagined. We offered him a little tiny container and he packed it full.

Then we have the other end of the continuum (the generous end). At that end I imagine my father-in-law's grain scoop. That is the biggest shovel I've ever seen in my life. If that grain scoop were used for dispensing love, when you filled it you'd have almost more love than you knew what to do with. God, in his nature, returns love to us in a grain scoop. He starts with a big container and then he presses it down so more will fit in. Then he gives it a shake so even more will fit. And finally he adds so much more that it runs over. That's a lot of love he's giving back.

Do you remember that I told you about a young girl killed shortly after she had heard the gospel message from one of her friends at an FCA meeting?

Her parents are givers. In the year following her death, her mother went out of her way to encourage the young girls who had been her daughter's friends. She attended their ballgames and "oohed" and "ahhed" over their prom dresses. Even in the midst of her personal tragedy, she chose to give encouragement to them.

Being a giver is a good choice for a positive attitude.

CHOOSE TO HOPE

Find rest, O my soul, in God alone;
my hope comes from him.
Psalm 62:5

Lynn lay in the hospital bed with bandages and tubes everywhere. I had been on a pretty predictable schedule of visiting her every other day since her surgery. The hospital was over an hour from our home, but the journey seemed insignificant. After all, I was visiting one of my dearest friends.

Lynn had been diagnosed with a brain tumor only two weeks before. The doctors had performed surgery and were not encouraged by the outcome. The tumor was not isolated. It had spread extensively, and even radiation was not expected to make a difference.

So every other day I found someone to watch my boys and I headed to Lynn's hospital room. There wasn't much I could accomplish on my visits. She was very tired and sedated, so I usually just sat by her bed and read to her from the Bible.

One day I took along a little devotional book I had picked up somewhere. It was based on Scripture, with over three hundred different meditations on the names of Jesus. The names were listed alphabetically and I began by fanning through the pages and reading one here and one there. "Jesus is the pearl of great price." "Jesus is our dwelling place." "Jesus is the spring of water." Though her eyes were open, Lynn lay motionless.

As I flipped through the pages I found a devotional entitled "Jesus is our healer." I was just sure that Lynn would respond to this page. Surely healer was the description of Jesus about which she longed to hear.

It was a beautiful devotion but my friend did not acknowledge it. Then I turned to the very next page and read, "Jesus is my hope."

As I read the page-long devotional, Lynn began to respond. She turned her head toward me and listened intently as I read about the hope we have in Jesus Christ.

When I finished the page she began to speak. Communication was very difficult for her and conversation was almost impossible, so I listened carefully.

"Again," she said weakly. "Again."

Lynn wanted me to read about hope once more.

On my drive home that day I thought about her request. "Again." She had wanted to hear again about the hope we have in Jesus.

> Now faith is being sure of what we hope for
> and certain of what we do not see.
> *Hebrews 11:1*

When there is no other thing for us to hold on to, there is hope. We can have hope in the eternal life with Jesus that is promised to all those who believe in him. Regardless of our circumstances, we can choose to hope. Lynn had chosen hope in Jesus—a hope that days later carried her to his waiting arms.

12

Choose Daily

> "But as for me and my household,
> we will serve the Lord."
> *Joshua 24:15b*

The Scripture above is often posted on doorposts and housefronts. It is a meaningful message, but I've always felt that the first part of the verse was potentially more significant than the last, more familiar part. "Choose for yourselves this day whom you will serve" (Joshua 24:15a).

We are instructed to choose *this day* whom we are going to serve. Choose today whom you are going to serve. And then choose again tomorrow. One good choice does not mean you are finished, it simply means you have made one good choice. You must follow that choice with the next right choice and the next right choice after that.

Even though the people you have read about have made good choices, choices that have led to a positive attitude, they did not make just one good choice. They have made consistent, consecutive good choices. Where are these heroines of the positive attitude now? Let's see.

Jean Driscoll (Choose to Have a Vision) ran her eighth Boston Marathon in the spring of 1997. At mile twenty-two, her wheel caught in a trolley track and she crashed while traveling twenty miles per hour. Fortunately, she suffered only minor scrapes. Her wheelchair was righted and she finished the race in second place. At the present time she is training for the 1998 Boston Marathon. Her vision? To set her eighth course and world record in 1998 and possibly even her ninth in 1999.

Sonnie (Choose to Respond) sold her flower shop after Eric's accident. She still works there two or three days a week. Eric has a job, too. For about three or four hours a week he works at the local bank, running the paper shredder. He loves his job and continues to be a blessing to all those around him. He recently celebrated his thirtieth birthday as the guest of honor at a surprise party.

Darla and her family (Choose to Be Flexible) continue to flourish. For five years after her graduation from nursing school, Darla served as the director of the nursing staff at an area nursing home. She recently received a promotion and is now working from her home as a consultant to a chain of nursing homes in her state.

Joan and Elizabeth (Choose to Be Content) both go to school each day. Joan is now teaching fourth grade. Besides giving of herself to her family and her students, Joan has found a niche in politics and is currently serving on the County Board. She is also a State Central Committeeman, a statewide office for her party. Since the age of two, Elizabeth has taken phenobarbitol for seizures. In August of 1997 she was able to stop taking the drug and has been seizure-free.

Betty (Choose Not to Worry) has recovered miraculously from the abuse she suffered for almost two decades. "I do not regret leaving," she told me. "I only regret that I didn't leave sooner for the sake of my children." Today Betty is married to a kind and gentle man. He is very caring and protective of her. "I am happy," Betty said. "I know that God provided for me and he continues to do so today."

Shirley's doctors told her in May of 1997 that she had only weeks to live (Choose Joy). She was instructed to plan her funeral and say good-bye to her family and friends. In October of 1997 we had lunch together. As we sat at the table marveling at what God had done, she told me that she had reordered her datebook subscription for 1998.

In January of 1998, Shirley entered the hospice program. She continues to encourage me with her joyful spirit as we visit by phone each week.

Pam's daughter, Emily (Choose to Pray), is cancer-free. She and her family recently visited Disney World, compliments of the Make-A-Wish Foundation. She also appeared at the halftime show of Monday Night Football to celebrate the twenty-year anniversary of the Ronald McDonald House. Each year Pam, Emily, and the rest of their family walk in a "long-term survivor" walk along Lake Shore Drive in Chicago to raise money for cancer research. And Pam is still praying.

It has been over eight years since *Amanda's* death and Jane's initial commitment to Christ (Choose Jesus). Jane and I did an early Sunday morning Bible study together for more than two years. Now she and her family attend Sunday school and church near their home and also go to a weekly "Logos Program" of Bible study, worship, and "family time." Her faith is strong and she lives it in her daily life.

My father has been gone more than twenty-three years (Choose to Forgive). I am very thankful that we had some degree of reconciliation before his death. I am also thankful that God has given me the choice not only to forgive, but also to ask for forgiveness. Life on earth is so very short. Choosing to ask for forgiveness can foster healing of relationships and a positive attitude.

> Every experience God gives us,
> every person He puts in our lives,
> is the perfect preparation
> for the future that only
> He can see.
> *Corrie ten Boom*

The choices we have in life are numerous. In fact, they are so abundant that there are very few things that are *not* our choice.

As a young girl I would try in vain to persuade my mother that I *had* to do something or other. To this she would consistently reply, "Kendra, there are only two things in life that you *have* to do. All the other things are choices. All you *have* to do is die and pay taxes!"

Maybe you heard that from your mother, too. Well, today, with respect, I would say to my 80+-year-old mother, "Actually, Mom, all you *have* to do is die." (Now before some IRS representative starts checking on my file, I want to make it perfectly clear that I have chosen to pay taxes each year of my adult life. Paying taxes is a very wise choice and it beats high fines and jail sentences. It is, however, a choice.)

Every woman in this book had choices to make. So do you. Our choices are infinite in number and they are our daily responsibility.

We can choose joy and forgiveness and Jesus and contentment and prayer. We can choose to be flexible, to respond, to have a vision, and not to worry. Or we can choose to let the "if only's" and "what if's" of life control us.

My goal is to make intentionally good choices for a positive life, just as these women did. My dream is to encourage you to do the same!

Notes

TWO
Choose to Forgive

1. Jane E. Brody, "Personal Health," *New York Times*, April 12, 1995, 13.

FIVE
Choose Joy

1. "A Chuckle a Day Does Indeed Help Keep Ills at Bay," *USA Today,* October 31, 1996, 10D.
2. "Happily Ever Laughter," *Psychology Today,* July 1996:32-35.
3. "Laughter, It's Good Medicine," *Better Homes and Gardens*, April 1997, 72.
4. "A Chuckle a Day Does Indeed Help Keep Ills at Bay," *USA Today,* October 31, 1996, 10D.
5. "Does God Have a Sense of Humor?" *Moody Monthly*, June 1987, 60-61.

SEVEN
Choose to Be Content

1. Elisabeth Kubler-Ross, *On Death and Dying* (New York: Macmillan, 1969), 39.